AFRICAN AMERICAN MEN AND THE POLICE

AFRICAN AMERICAN MEN AND THE POLICE

A Christ Solution for the New Millennium

Reverend Dr. Maulin Chris Herring

Copyright © 2015 Reverend Dr. Maulin Chris Herring

All rights reserved.

ISBN-13: 9781517302788
ISBN-10: 1517302781
Library of Congress Control Number: 2015915038
CreateSpace Independent Publishing Platform
North Charleston, South Carolina

DEDICATION

In memory of my mother, Hazel Bezel Carr Herring, who provided her sons with the foundational opportunity to develop their personal relationship with Christ and watered that seed until her homegoing celebration. Mom sacrificed everything, with the exception of her personal relationship with Christ, for her three sons. In memory of my grandfather, the Reverend Robert Leslie Carr, who took the time to teach me how a man of God should live life, and who gave me the love that every young Black male should receive from a man.

TABLE OF CONTENTS

Acknowledgments · xi
Definition of Terms · xiii
Abstract · xv
African American Men and the Police: A Christ Solution
for the New Millennium · xv
Introduction · xvii
Hypothesis · xvii
Research Methodologies · xxi
Limitations and Delimitations · xxi
Chapter 1 Spiritual Autobiography · 1
First Impressions of the Police · 2
Grandfather's Mentoring · 3
Introduction to Law Enforcement · 4
Law Enforcement Management · 5
Black Men and Police Relations · 6
Cup of Salvation Deliverance Church and Ministries · · · · · · · 7
Durham City Demographics and Crime · · · · · · · · · · · · · · · · 9
Durham City Crime · 9
Durham Community Relationships with Police · · · · · · · · · · 10
Chapter 2 Statement of the Problem · 13
Sources for Current Statistics and Research · · · · · · · · · · · · · 16
Chapter 3 Foundations · 18
Biblical Foundations · 18
Biblical Foundations Introduction · 19
Old Testament Foundation-Exodus 2 · · · · · · · · · · · · · · · · · 20

Verse 11	22
Verse 12	24
Verse 13	24
Verse 14	25
Verse 15	26
New Testament Foundation-Luke 22	28
Jesus and Roman Authority	29
Verse 47	33
Verse 48	34
Verse 49	34
Verse 50	34
Verse 51	35
Verse 52	36
Theological Foundation: Practical Theology	37
Historical/Contemporary Foundations	48
The Church and Social Justice	48
African Americans' Historical Perception of Law Enforcement	55
Churches and Black Community/Law Enforcement Engagement	58
US Department of Justice Office Community Oriented Policing Services	59
Black Males and Police Relations	61
Theoretical Foundation	64

Chapter 4

Research Methodologies	67
Field Experience-Implementing The Program	69
Bible Study	70
Sermon	71
Workshop Recruitment	72
Men's Ministry Meeting Discussion	73
Workshop	73
Workshop Material	74
Room Design	75

	Workshop Delivery	76
	Focus Group Discussion	83
	My Assessment	84
	Workshop Data Analysis	85
	Summary	90
	Focus Group Discussion Analysis	90
	Case Study	93
	Participant Background	93
	Development of Attitude Toward Police	94
	Workshop Strengths	94
	Recommended Potential Changes to Workshop	94
	Notable Statements	94
	Overall Findings	95
	Relevant Information Learned	95
	Participants' Opinions Changed after the Workshop	96
	Value of Workshop	96
	Recommended Changes to Workshop	97
	Roundtable Discussion with Law Enforcement	97
Chapter 5	Summary, Conclusions, Recommendations	100
	What did I learn about myself during this study?	100
	What did I learn about the people associated with this study?	100
	What happened that was unexpected?	101
	What would I do differently?	101
	Potential Next Steps for Your Church	102
	Workshops with Christians	102
	Workshops with Law Enforcement	102
	Prayer and Bible Study	103
	Local Law Enforcement and Community Engagement	103
	Law Enforcment Organizational Transformation and Strategic Community Engagement	104
	Ex-Offender Community Re-entry	104
	Conclusion	105

Appendices · 107
    Appendix A. Sermon: Moses and the Plight of Young
        Black Men in the United States
        and Authority · 109
    Appendix B. CSDC Bible Study 10/25/13 · · · · · · · · · · · · · · · 115
    Appendix C. Workshop Announcement Flyer · · · · · · · · · · · 118
    Appendix D. Workshop Handouts · · · · · · · · · · · · · · · · · · · 120
    Workshop Agenda · 120
    Consent Form · 122
        Consent to Participate in Research · · · · · · · · · · · · · · 122
    Pre/Post Surveys · 125
        PRE SURVEY · 125
        POST SURVEY · 127
    Robbins's Christian Authority Article · · · · · · · · · · · · · · · · 129
    Black Criminal Stereotypes and Racial Profiling · · · · · · · · · 129
    Workshop Evaluation (Small Group Session) · · · · · · · · · · · · · 130
        WORKSHOP EVALUATION · 130
    Appendix E. Small Group Transcription · · · · · · · · · · · · · · · 131
    Appendix F. Case Study Interview Transcription · · · · · · · · · 138
    Appendix G. E-mail Invitation to Law Enforcement
        to Attend Roundtable Discussion · · · · · · · · · · · · 144
    Appendix H. Annotated Bibliography · · · · · · · · · · · · · · · · · 146
    Biblical · 146
    Theological · 148
    Historical · 150
    Contemporary · 151
    Research · 155
    About the Author · 157
    Bibliography · 159

ACKNOWLEDGMENTS

I WOULD LIKE TO take this moment to thank those who have helped to make this doctor of ministry project possible and those who have supported this lifelong learner on a mountain climb to intimacy that has strengthened and prepared me to play yet a stronger role in the building of His kingdom. I thank APEX School of Theology under the powerful spiritual leadership of Dr. Joseph Perkins for accepting me in the doctor of ministry program, and all of the school's faculty and staff.

I am especially appreciative to Dr. Lafayette Maxwell as dean of the doctor of ministry program and Dr. Terry Thomas, who stepped in to make completion possible. I give a heart-filled thanks and appreciation to the Cup of Salvation Deliverance Church family under the spiritual leadership of Apostle Dr. Johnny Holloway. I thank the "Cup" Men's Ministry and Executive Pastor, Versal Mason (who served as context associate); Executive Pastor, Deborah Holloway; and Elder James Robertson and Elder Charles Freeman for allowing me to use the men's ministry as a sample population of context. I give many thanks to Dr. Kenethia Fuller for her research design and statistical analysis oversight. I thank Ms. Diane Sampson for her many hours of editing.

I give a heartfelt thanks to those special and select family members and friends who supported me with prayer and a word of encouragement at just the right time. Enough thanks and acknowledgment cannot be expressed to my loving family for their patience and support. Without their love and understanding, this journey would not have been completed. All praises and thanks go to my Heavenly Father for making everything possible.

DEFINITION OF TERMS

DEFINING TERMS MAKES it possible for readers to have a clear understanding of the key concepts discussed in this book. The definition below may not be a dictionary definition, but it is one that helps to clarify the ideas of this project. Here are a few definitions that may assist with clarity and understanding.

African American and Black: The terms *African American* and *Black* are used interchangeably and refer to women and men in the United States who have a heritage of slavery and origins from Africa. This is relevant due to the generational experiences and impacts that have been passed down. Considering and respecting the rich history of the mixing of races in the United States, the premise of Shaun Gabbidon and Helen Green is adopted.[1] The individual makes his or her decision on what race he or she claims.

At risk: The term *at risk* refers to youth who live in certain conditions that make them more susceptible to victimization and delinquency. This includes a combination of social conditions, such as poverty, crime, limited family support, peer association, and poor education performance, to name a few.

authority: For the purpose of this study, *authority* is the power or right to control, judge, or prohibit the actions of others.[2] The English version of the New

---

1 Shaun Gabbidon, L. and Helen Taylor Greene. *Race and Crime.* Thousand Oaks, CA: Sage Publications, Inc., 2005.
2 Authority. Dictionary.com. *Collins English Dictionary: Complete & Unabridged 10th Edition.* HarperCollins Publishers. http://dictionary.reference.com/browse/authorities (accessed: November 9, 2014).

Testament translates the Greek *exousia*, a word for which there is no exact correspondence in Hebrew or Aramaic, using the word authority. The Greek *exousia* expresses both freedom and legal rights, and is used in the Bible in numerous ways.[3]

carnal minded: *Carnal minded* refers to viewing life, experiences, and perceptions from the worldly perspective of humankind. Romans 8:5–8 provides biblical insight: For they that are after the flesh do mind the things of the flesh; but they that are after the Spirit the things of the Spirit. For to be carnally minded is death; but to be spiritually minded is life and peace. Because the carnal mind is enmity against God: for it is not subject to the law of God, neither indeed can be. So then they that are in the flesh cannot please God.[4]

spiritual minded: *Spiritual minded* refers to viewing everything from a Christlike perspective.

mentor: In this book, the term *mentor* refers to a broader base of one person communicating with another person, informally or formally, in the long term or short term, with the purpose of changing his or her perceptions and actions.

---

[3] Trent Butler, Editor. Entry for "Authority." Holman Bible Dictionary. http://www.studylight.org/dictionaries/hbd/view.cgi?n=566. 1991.
[4] Romans 8:5–8.

ABSTRACT

AFRICAN AMERICAN MEN AND THE POLICE: A CHRIST SOLUTION FOR THE NEW MILLENNIUM

I designed a systematic approach that introduced biblical principles and a spiritual foundation for training men to educate and mentor African American young men. The goal of this training was to develop positive relationships with law enforcement with the ultimate goal of reducing aggressive law enforcement encounters, controlling crime in the community, and changing criminal justice policy. Practical theology and cultural conflict theory are used as the foundations. This project entailed a sermon, a Bible study, a roundtable discussion among Christian men, a workshop that targeted spiritual understanding of Christian men and the police's authority, and a roundtable discussion with local law enforcement representatives. This model relies heavily on addressing the social phenomenon from a spiritual minded approach rather than a carnal minded approach. Men who attended the training and discussions increased their understanding of African American men and police relations in the United States, and the need to educate African American men and police on how to improve relationships via Christian principles, leading to positive community encounters while influencing the criminal justice system. Law enforcement officers who attended the roundtables gained insight into why Black men have negative perceptions of law enforcement. The ultimate goal was to develop an evidence-based model that can be duplicated throughout the United States.

INTRODUCTION

HYPOTHESIS

If Christian men are reminded of and educated on Biblical concepts of mentoring, faith, how the community would benefit from positive police collaboration, and steps to take when approached by police, then they will be more motivated and empowered to mentor young African American men on how to avoid conflict with law enforcement and improve law enforcement relations using the methods taught by their Christian mentors.

This book is based on a dissertation for a Doctor of Ministry degree at Apex School of Theology in Durham, North Carolina. Since the primary intended audience is not the academic community, I made several adjustments to make the book more appropriate for members of the faith community. While challenging, I also wanted to maintain the scholarly research foundations for those in the theological and academic communities.

The purpose of this study was to develop a model Christian-based curriculum that allows the church to serve as a catalyst in mentoring Black males to strengthen relationships with the criminal justice system from a spiritual minded perspective. The curriculum will teach Christians to assess the social factors that influence their perceptions of police, and how these perceptions may influence police encounters. Influencing young Black men's perceptions from a Christ perspective may be accomplished by providing training to Christian men. These Christian men would then educate young Black males on how to interact with police while increasing trust and changing policy.

It must be acknowledged that law enforcement also have a responsibility when it comes to improving the relationship between them and Black men. While this project focuses on measures Black males control, there continues to be a gap in evidence based programs designed to change the perceptions and actions of police when dealing with Black men.

While it is limited, research addressing the issue of religion and crime is not new. Scott and Morgan cite that Black Protestant congregations are culturally committed to the inner city, and outreach to poor urban neighborhoods is important to them.[5] They also mention that Black Protestant congregations are engaged in their neighborhoods with an emphasis on helping the underprivileged.

In the article *When 2 or 3 Come Together*,[6] the authors research the benefits and constitutionality of churches partnering with police to address issues of crime in poor neighborhoods. Their study resulted from a community-wide prayer vigil held in Chicago in 1997 that resulted from the collaboration between the Chicago Police Department and hundreds of mostly Black churches on Chicago's West Side. The article confirms that churches and government (police) can be successful when collaborating to address issues of crime in Black communities, but there are some constitutional implications of religion and state that may need to be considered.

There is a gap in research that explores how Christian men perceive the development of their attitudes toward police. There is also a gap in reseach that explores how Christian men perceive what role their attitudes toward police may play in armoring young Black males on how to improve their perception of police and what to do when encountered by police. Armoring refers to the intergenerational transferring of information about police from the parent to the child.[7] In their research findings, Meares and Corkan suggest that

---

5 Desmond Scott and Kristopher H. Morgan. "Congregations and Crime: Is the Spatial Distribution of Congregations Associated with Neighborhood Crime Rates?" *Journal For The Scientific Study Of Religion* 49, No. 1 (2010): 37–55.

6 Tracey Meares and Kelsi B. Corkan. "When 2 Or 3 Come Together." *William And Mary Law Review* 48, No. 4 (2007): 1315–1387.

7 Rod Brunson and Ronald Weitzer. "Negotiating Unwelcome Police Encounters: The Intergenerational Transmission of Conduct Norms." *Journal Of Contemporary Ethnography* 40, No. 4 (2011): 425–456.

Black parents educate their sons about police and police encounters, but primarily on the basis of fear and distrust. The authors provide a "tool kit" of information on what young Black males should do when they encounter the police, with recommendations for avoiding them. Some of these findings were used in the development of the workshop utilized for this study.

This gap in research is extended when one considers basing the "armoring" of young Black men on police relationships with foundations from Christian principles and Christian mentoring. This project uses the mentoring concepts of Christ as discussed in *Mentor Like Jesus*.[8] When Christian men prepare to educate young Black males about police relations, a foundation of spiritual concepts should be presented. Campbell and Chaney provide eleven characteristics of what they call "next generation mentors":[9]

1. It is on purpose.
2. It is a selfless endeavor.
3. It starts in a group context.
4. It involves handpicked mentorees.
5. It is for a defined period of time.
6. It is centered on truth.
7. It involves the practice of prayer.
8. It requires transparent modeling.
9. It incorporates a contextual component.
10. It demands mutual commitment.
11. It requires a multiplication element.

This study and intervention uses the concept of mentoring to describe formal and informal conversations that Christian men should have to educate young Black males about police relations and encounters. To address the problem of young Black males' negative perceptions of police, short informational conversations to structured educational initiatives are needed. While there are

---

8 Regi Campbell and Richard Chancy. *Mentor Like Jesus*. Nashville, TN: B&H Publishing Group, 2009.
9 Ibid.

many programs that are designed to improve relationships between the Black community and police, none have been identified that specifically focus on the Christian principles of the lifelong journey of mentoring that is pursued from the heart as discussed in *The Heart of Mentoring: Ten Proven Principles for Developing People to their Fullest Potential.*[10] There is a need to educate and mentor Christian men who will then educate and mentor young Black males on how to strengthen relationships with police and the criminal justice system.

There is an assumption that men who profess to be Christians have accepted Jesus Christ as their Lord and Savior and are at different points in their spiritual journey, or in their personal relationship with Christ. There is also an assumption that Black males have a very high level of distrust of police. This is an emotional issue to many of them and it will take the power of the Holy Spirit to provide guidance.

Without question, women have played and must continue to play a significant role in strengthening relationships between the African American community and the criminal justice system. Curriculum can and should include women, especially considering their historical role of raising young Black males. I focused on Black men to narrow the population for the original research design and population.

This book is divided into five chapters: 1) spiritual autobiography; 2) statement of the problem; 3) foundations; 4) research methodologies; and 5) conclusions. Chapter one discusses my personal, professional and spiritual journeys which have led to my subject matter expertise. Chapter one also provides insight to the context, or location selected for the study. Chapter two provides an overview of the problem, demonstrating a need for a different approach to bring about change. Chapter three is an important chapter in that it provides scriptural exegisis, theological foundations, a review of relevant literature and theoretical foundations to support and better understand the depth and scope of the problem, as well was the recommended solution. Chapter four includes the research design, curriculum design, field

---

10 David Stoddard, A. and Robert Tamasy. *The Heart Of Mentoring: Ten Proven Principles for Developing People to Their Fullest Potential.* Colorado Springs, CO: Navpress, 2010.

experience and findings. In this chapter you will find the actual program that could be modeled within your community. It is located in the section, Field Experience-Implementing the Program. Chapter five serves as the conclusion and summarizes the study, providing my personal reflection and important potential next steps that readers can consider. Also included at the end is an appendix. The appendix includes copies of handouts and other information used in the project. Some of the copies included are a sermon and information shared at a bible study to begin informing a larger section of the congregation.

RESEARCH METHODOLOGIES

A triangulation research design composed of pre/post surveys, small group discussion, and a case study was used.[11] A panel discussion with local law enforcement representatives was added after the original research design to gain more insight into law enforcement and Black male relationships at a micro level. I observed and documented attitudinal changes that came from members and visitors of the Men's Ministry at Cup of Salvation Deliverance Church and Ministries. An ethnographic approach is used to study participants' interest and ability to mentor young Black men on how to improve relationships with police based on Christian principles.[12]

LIMITATIONS AND DELIMITATIONS

As with most research projects; there are limitations and delimitations. Limitations are those things that I could not control. The limitations include convenience sampling (using the Men's Ministry that was already established), sample size, questionnaire pre/post comparisons, and time limitations. Since convenience sampling was used rather than random sampling, findings cannot be generally applied, but rather suggested. The sample size of twenty-one

---

11 Bruce Berg. *Qualitative Research Methods for the Social Sciences.* Boston: Pearson, 2007.
12 Kenneth Bordens and Bruce Abbott. *Research Design and Methods: A Process Approach.* Boston: McGraw-Hill, 2005.

is rather limiting. A final limitation is the lack of control for participants who came late, stayed for the full workshop and fully completed the pre- and post questionnaires, giving their names. Those participants that came late were not influenced by the full session and the levels of changes that were measured at the end may have been impacted. Since some participants left early, they did not take the post test and that limited the total number that took the pre and post test for analysis. Considering these limitations, using triangulation strengthens the findings.

Delimitations are things that I had control of and the boundaries that I set for this study. There are two primary delimitations for the project: the context (City of Durham, NC) and the focus on attitudinal changes of Black males. Another delimitation is the choice to focus on changing the views and actions of Christian Black men who can then educate and influence the views and actions of young Black males in the community. There is acknowledgment that attitudinal change must also take place with police. The focus on Black male attitudinal change was due to the desire to give them immediate control of their own actions and responses to police encounters.

1

SPIRITUAL AUTOBIOGRAPHY

WHAT MAKES REVEREND Dr. Maulin Chris Herring an appropriate change agent for engaging the church to strengthen the relationship among Black men, law enforcement, and the criminal justice system from a spiritual-minded approach? All too often, individuals appoint themselves as champions for a cause. One must first seek God personally when deciding to impact the community with commitment and intent to bring about change and justice. Every battle is not for every person, and every person is not for every battle. It is clear that God purposed me for this time, this occasion, and this cause. When determining purpose, especially for social justice causes, one should seek God and reflect on why the mission is his or hers. Here is the journey God allowed that led to this project of developing a model program that uses the church to strengthen the relationship among Black men, police, and the criminal justice system. Anyone who endeavors to embark on a similar destiny should consider examining her or his own journey that has prepared her or him for a similar call for justice.

I was born in Los Angeles, California in 1960. More specifically, I was raised in Pacoima in the San Fernando Valley. Pacoima was a multicultural community made up of primarily Black, Mexican, and White residents. My parents separated when I was about four years old and divorced when I was about six. I do not recall my father ever living in the house with us while growing up in California. I did not see him or hear from him again after the age of six until I was a rookie police officer in North Carolina at age twenty-two.

My mother raised three sons in the streets of L.A., and I was the youngest of the three siblings. Mom, a nurse, often worked third shift, 11:00 p.m. to 7:00 a.m. With a strong southern rural Baptist upbringing and as the middle daughter (of seven) of a North Carolina preacher/farmer, mom kept her boys active in church. As a child, I attended Greater Community Baptist Church under the leadership of the late Reverend T.G. Pledger. My brothers and I attended Sunday school and Sunday service on a regular basis. Even if Mom worked Saturday night, getting off early Sunday morning, too tired to go to church, she made sure someone picked us up and took us to church. I grew up participating in the traditional Easter and Christmas programs, reciting biblical scriptures and poems, and participating in plays. Everyone knew the Herring boys and Greater Community Baptist Church was a comfortable second home.

FIRST IMPRESSIONS OF THE POLICE

My first memory of the police includes three incidents. I remember a fight on one of the corners at the intersection of Paxton Street and Glenoaks Boulevard in Pacoima. A large crowd gathered around. This was a major intersection with a gas station about a block from my house. I was far toward the back of the crowd and noticed a police car drive by. I did not understand why the police did not stop to break up the fight. I was about eight years old at the time. The police saw the guys seriously "going at it." They saw the big crowd, and yet, they drove by.

My next police memory took place at a park next to Pacoima Elementary School. It is actually the absence of police that makes the event so memorable. Apparently, someone had run into the rear end of a Black male's car. The Black male had the man who hit his car pinned down in the front seat of his own car, just beating him in the face. When he let the guy up for a couple of minutes, there was the largest amount of blood I had ever seen on the guy. I mean the guy's shirt was soaked and his face was all bloody. As I recall, the man being beaten was Mexican. This beating went on for what seemed to be a pretty long time, at least to me as a young man under the age of ten. Watching through the fence at the edge of the park along with a pretty large crowd, I thought, *Where are the police?*

And finally, school uprisings that spilled into neighborhoods were a thing of the era. The police must have anticipated one on this particular day. As my mother, my middle brother, and I drove home, the police cars were lined up all along the street. Nothing ever happened, but just seeing so many police cars lined up along the street sticks in my mind still today.

My mother always made it very clear to me not to trust the police and stay away from them. She often said, "Once they get your name, they will never leave you alone." This came from a single mom who was determined to protect her sons. Raising three boys alone, Mom soon decided to head back east and we moved to North Carolina.

GRANDFATHER'S MENTORING

My grandfather, the late Reverend Robert Leslie Carr, was a rural North Carolina preacher and farmer. For more than thirty years, he pastored four churches at one time, ministering on rotating Sundays. Granddaddy had an elementary school education, but had attended pastoral continuing education training throughout North Carolina in his adult years, including at Shaw Divinity School. He was very active with the Lott Carey Convention and many other Baptist associations. Granddaddy retired in the late '70s, when he was still preaching at three churches. He answered his call into ministry in his early twenties. He was born in the late 1890s. He served as a pastor for more than fifty years. Each of his last four churches still exists today. The one in Fayetteville, Lewis Chapel, is one of Cumberland County's largest, with a senior citizen residential complex and a school. I remember when Granddaddy assisted and approved of the selection of his replacement pastor, Reverend Dr.

J.D. Fuller. The late Reverend R.L. Carr, my grandfather, significantly influenced my spiritual growth, as well as my development as a young Black man.

While I thought Granddaddy was exclusively mine, I later discovered that many of my cousins, female and male, had similar and even stronger personal relationships with him. Granddaddy had a way of making you feel like you were his special and favorite grandchild. These experiences with my grandfather and the spiritual growth I experienced served as a foundation for future life experiences. Little did I know how much they would aid me in my career and my growing relationship with and dependency on Christ.

INTRODUCTION TO LAW ENFORCEMENT

At age 20, in 1981, I became a Chapel Hill, North Carolina public safety officer (firefighter, EMT, and police officer). I was clueless and probably a little hesitant; I only knew I needed a job. As I understand it, I was number eight out of the seven people hired. Six Whites and one Black person were scheduled to start the class. The other Black male who had been hired had some problems that came up. I became the only Black Chapel Hill public safety officer in the Chapel Hill Police Department's first public safety academy. I entered at a time when the Black officers were suing the department for discriminatory acts.

As a young police officer, after seeing the many young Black males in the community and their plight, a special "tug" that I cannot explain started within me whenever I saw their many encounters with police. While on the job, I remember hearing about a meeting after hours in the courthouse that was called by Judge Stanley Peele. The meeting was to start a mentoring program for "at risk" youth. I am not sure why, but I was drawn to go to the meeting and I felt a sense of responsibility to be involved. At the time I was about twenty-one years old. That organization became Volunteers For Youth. Over about a seven-year span, I was a mentor to four young Black males and eventually served on the advisory board.

I stayed with most of the young brothers beyond the one-year commitment. I would occasionally get calls late at night when one of them was in trouble and often would be called upon to act as their spokesperson in formal proceedings. Neighboring city Durham had Durham Companions as its Big Brother/Big Sister program, and I eventually served on its advisory board as well. The Big Brother/Sister programs always struggled to get Black males to serve as mentors. White males frequently volunteered and always made up the majority of Big Brothers, while the majority of the boys were Black. I continued to formally and informally mentor young men after the age of fifty and participated in a mentoring program called Tarheel Challenge Academy, run by the state of North Carolina and sponsored by the National Guard.

After three and a half years as a Chapel Hill public safety officer, I knew I needed to finish my education. I never fell in love with the job, like some officers who needed it to define who they were. I decided to take a cut in pay and go over to the University of North Carolina (UNC) Police Department. While with the UNC Police Department, and during my time as a full-time student at North Carolina Central University (NCCU) at the age of twenty-five, I was assigned to a countywide drug task force that was coordinated by the N.C. State Bureau of Investigations. I was introduced to undercover operations and buying small amounts of drugs. Working with this unit actually helped me attain the flexibility I needed to pursue a Bachelor of Arts degree (BA). I went to classes during the day and worked on drug investigations in the late afternoon and evening. The degree and experiences did not help me with my first law enforcement promotion process. I filed discrimination charges against the UNC Police Department.

LAW ENFORCEMENT MANAGEMENT

In Decatur, Illinois, I served as the support services manager in the Safety Services Department (police and fire), which was equivalent to a deputy chief in the fire and police departments. As a civilian, I was the highest-ranking Black person in both departments at the age of thirty. I later became the interim director of the North Carolina Community Policing Center, hired directly by the North Carolina Secretary of Crime Control and Public Safety. Eventually, I became the first Black police chief in two communities, Hartsville, South

Carolina and Salisbury, North Carolina. During this short span of about twelve years, I became known as a national consultant in the area of community engagement and law enforcement. My primary area of expertise was cultural diversity. I spoke at numerous law enforcement conferences throughout the United States, consulting for leading national law enforcement organizations like the International Association of Chiefs of Police, National Sherriff's Association, and the National Organization of Black Law Enforcement Executives. I provided training and consultation to numerous law enforcement agencies and hundreds of personnel in the areas of diversity, ethics, community problem solving, management principles, and organizational behavior. I have facilitated training in nearly every state in the nation.

BLACK MEN AND POLICE RELATIONS

By this point in my life, I had developed a passion for the support and success of young "at risk" Black males. I had supported a number of programs and served as an activist for this cause. In Decatur, I became active in the Black community and consulted with the police command staff on Black community relations during a time of, let us say, strain and challenges. I was asked to speak with "problem" young Black men in elementary schools and volunteered with the Boys and Girls Club. In Hartsville, I led the start of a Boys and Girls Club of America, started a group of men called *Concerned Citizens* who walked the drug and crime areas, and started a Police Youth Academy for "at risk" youth. In Hartsville, I also started an aggressive community policing initiative where the police would meet with neighborhood groups. In Salisbury, I mandated police officer foot patrols to get closer to the community, aggressively spoke at neighborhood meetings, invited in community representatives to officer hiring/promotion meetings, and started a group called *Black and Blue*. The group was composed of diverse Black males and police who met to discuss concerns and relations.

Like many people, I submitted to God's call into ministry after trials and tribulations. Interestingly enough, mine took place as I was aggressively attempting to bring about organizational and community change in local law enforcement. Dr. Nilous Avery II and Mt. Zion Missionary Baptist church were there to shepherd us through. I was licensed and ordained in the General Baptist State Convention of North Carolina-Rowan Baptist Association. Later, I was installed as Elder and then Associate Pastor at Cup of Salvation Deliverance Church and Ministries in Durham, North Carolina under the leadership of Apostle Dr. Johnny Holloway.

CUP OF SALVATION DELIVERANCE CHURCH AND MINISTRIES

When making the prayerful decision to improve the quality of life in a community, it is important for the initiator(s) to assess and reflect on the church and the community, as well. Several questions must be asked:

- Why are we committing to this?
- Does it align with our doctrine?
- What do we absolutely and specifically know about the community, law enforcement and crime?

Too often, church organizations and leaders engage in social justice initiatives without seeking God first and truly assessing if the cause is their calling. The following is the assessment and reflection for this project, which is considered the contextual analysis.

Cup of Salvation Deliverance Church is in need of a men's ministry that understands they can have a positive impact on the city of Durham and the area surrounding the church. This is the area the church will focus on strengthening (Lazarus Territory). The church has an active men's ministry, but some of the men do not have a positive perception of police and have not reached out to "at risk" young men in the community, especially those who have a higher chance of having encounters with law enforcement. The men are in need of a ***spiritual minded*** approach to educating African American men, as well as the police, on strengthening African American young men and police relations in an attempt to reduce arrests, negative encounters, and prison recidivism. The men also need to be educated on measures they can employ to improve the criminal justice system.

The following information was retrieved from the church website.[13] Within a relatively short time span of just seventeen years, Cup of Salvation Deliverance Church & Ministries, Inc. (CSDC) has grown to be a spiritual force in the Durham community. CSDC was born in the heart of its founding pastor, Apostle Dr. Johnny Holloway, in 1992, but it did not officially open its doors until March 2, 1996. The name Cup of Salvation derives from Psalm 116:13: "I will take the cup of salvation and call upon the name of the Lord." For the first few weeks, the church of eight members met at the Hampton Inn on Hillandale Road, which fulfilled a prophecy God gave to Apostle Holloway while he and then Elder Deborah Holloway sat in their car in the parking lot of the Pan Pan restaurant adjacent to the hotel. In June 1996, the church moved to North Pointe Plaza on Guess Road, a location they fondly referred to as the "baby crib." Members often prayed that God would expand their horizons and perhaps give His baby church a "play pen" or even a "nursery" in which to grow. God moved and so did the church. On September 7, 1997, the congregation celebrated the first service at the current location at 1020 Highway 70 East, Durham. It is here that the church was first referred to as "The Cup," an endearment that most likely came from one of the early teenage members.

Cup of Salvation Deliverance Church and Ministries is a territorial, last days, apostolic ministry of warfare and deliverance. It is territorial in that members openly claim the Durham region for God, are willing to submit themselves to His will, and subject themselves to His Spirit so that the Durham region will be won for God. The Durham region is considered the city of Durham and the immediate surrounding areas. The Cup's mission is to "reach them, teach them, and set them free," as defined by Apostle Holloway. The intent is to take the city of Durham and the surrounding region from the grips of sin, despair, and oppression and convert it into a city that loves and serves God.[14]

This doctor of ministry research project was facilitated in coordination with the Cup Men's Ministry. The Men's Fellowship meets monthly on the first Saturday of each month at 10:00 a.m. Executive Pastor Versal Mason

---

13 Cup of Salvation website. Retrieved from http://cupofsalvation.org/.
14 Cup of Salvation Church and Ministries. Retrieved from http://cupofsalvation.org/.

serves as the fellowship pastor, while Associate Minister James H. Robertson Jr. is the director. Toward the end of this project, the leadership transferred to Pastor Deborah Holloway and Elder Charles Freeman.

DURHAM CITY DEMOGRAPHICS AND CRIME

The following information was retrieved from the *2012 Youth and Crime Community Indicator Report*.[15] Durham is the home of Research Triangle Park, Duke University, and North Carolina Central University. Located 406 feet above sea level, Durham County covers approximately 286 square miles. According to the 2010 census, Durham County is home to 267,587 residents, a 20 percent increase from 2000. It is a racially and ethnically diverse community, with 38 percent of Durham County residents are African American, and more than 13 percent are of Hispanic or Latino origin. Reflecting this diversity, Durham is the only county in the Triangle where the majority of the youth population is of a minority race. According to the American Community Survey (2010), 40 percent of Durham children live in single-family households (66 percent for Black/African American children). The state average is 34 percent.

DURHAM CITY CRIME

Risk factors in the community context include the availability of drugs, the presence of many neighborhood youth who are in trouble, the youths' feelings of being unsafe in the neighborhood, low levels of neighborhood integration, low neighborhood attachment, area poverty, and neighborhood disorganization. In Durham, as elsewhere, the underlying driver for most risk factors is family and neighborhood level poverty.

---

15 Gang Reduction Strategy Steering Committee, 2012 Youth and Crime Community Indicator Report. Retrieved from http://dconc.gov/government/departments-a-e/criminal-justice-resource-center/gang-reduction-strategy

Violent crime, especially violent crime committed by those below the age of 25, is of particular concern to the Durham community. Violent Part 1 crimes include murder, rape, and various forms of robbery and assault. According to the Durham Police Department, there were 1,771 Part 1 crimes committed in Durham in the three years ending December 31, 2011. Part 1 crimes by individuals under the age of 20, compared to arrests of all ages, are as follows:

2009: 22.1 percent
2010: 23.0 percent
2011: 18.4 percent

The number of Part 1 Violent Crimes in 2009, 2010, and 2011 increases to the age of sixteen, with a spike at age twenty-one. In 2009 and 2010, the spike occurred at the age of nineteen and eighteen, respectively, and in 2011 it occurred at age twenty-one. These statistics show that young people under the age of twenty are responsible for a large percent of Durham's most violent crimes. From this correlation, one can infer that these youth have encounters with police that have the potential to be aggressive.

DURHAM COMMUNITY RELATIONSHIPS WITH POLICE

There have been a number of community meetings, editorials, and reports that discuss strained relationships with police and the Black community in Durham. Brock & Meese Law Firm, which represents many Black defendants, state on its website that Black motorists are more than 200 percent more likely to be searched by law enforcement as a result of routine traffic stops for speeding, seat belt, and stop sign violations and that Black suspects are nearly nine times more likely to be incarcerated for criminal conduct than White suspects.[16] According to the website, Blacks arrested for drug crimes are nine times more likely to be incarcerated than White suspects;

---

16 Brock & Meese Law Firm. Retrieved from http://brockmeece.com/end-racial-profiling-in-durham-now/.

Hispanics are 3.8 times more likely to be incarcerated for drug crimes than White residents, and Blacks are 13.6 times more likely to be designated as a habitual felon.[17]

According to an article in the *Durham Herald Sun* (5/21/2014) titled *Blacks Suffer Disproportionately from Crime*:[18]

> While its true blacks in Durham are searched and arrested out of proportion to their share of the overall population, they're also the victims of crime more often than other ethnic groups, Police Department commanders state.
>
> That pattern holds in all five of the department's patrol districts, and is especially true for violent crimes like homicide, rape, robbery and aggravated assault, they said in a new report to the city's Human Relations Commission.

The report continued the department's response to allegations of racial profiling lodged by groups like the Southern Coalition for Social Justice and the Durham chapter of the NAACP.[19]

It is important to note that while the focus is often on aggressive police interactions, most statistics show that Black men are killed and injured mostly by other Black men. The *Durham Herald Sun* article goes on to state:

> Looking only at homicides, rapes, robberies and aggravated assaults, blacks were the victims in 66 percent of District 1's cases, 57 percent of District 2's, 48 percent of District 3's, 77 percent of District 4's and 60 percent of District 5's.[20]

---

17 Ibid.
18 Ray Gronberg. "Blacks Suffer Disproportionately from Crime." Retrieved from http://www.heraldsun.com/news/x112098135/Blacks-suffer-disproportionately-from-crime-police-say.
19 Ibid.
20 Ibid.

Christian men can have an impact on this critical phenomenon of Black on Black crime as well. Strengthening the relationship between Black men and police in the Durham community may have a residual impact on reducing Black male victimization at the hands of other Black men.

In an article posted on TV station WNCN's website posted on May 22, 2014, the headline read: *Durham mayor: Racial profiling report will not be 'gathering dust.*[21] The article discussed a report by several community groups addressing the race issues between the minority community and the Durham Police Department.

---

21 WNCN. "Durham mayor: Racial profiling report will not be gathering dust." Retrieved from http://www.wncn.com/story/25594185/durham-city-council-reviews-findings-of-racial-profiling-report.

2

STATEMENT OF THE PROBLEM

PROBLEM: YOUNG BLACK males between the ages of sixteen and twenty-one have a negative perception of law enforcement, and it may negatively impact their encounters with law enforcement officers, resulting in arrests, citations, injuries, and/or death.

Historically, in Great Britain as well as the United States, Blacks and police have had a difficult relationship full of social conflict and resulting in the distrust of police. This relationship of social conflict has roots in the oppressive nature of governments, once practiced by both countries. In Great Britain and the United States, this distrust resulted in communities' collective violent actions in resistance to oppressive state practices (riots).[22]

Direct or indirect contact with police may impact Blacks' perceptions of them and have an impact on the level of citizens' cooperation in assisting police with crime control measures in the community. As a result, negative perceptions of police may instigate scenarios that lead to arrests and hinder crime control measures that would lead to the increase in the number of

---

[22] Tendayi Viki, Michelle J. Culmer, Anja Eller, and Dominic Abrams. "Race and Willingness to Cooperate with the Police: The Roles of Quality of Contact, Attitudes Towards the Behavior and Subjective Norms." *British Journal of Social Psychology*, 20206: 285–302.

incarcerations. According to the Bureau of Justice Statistics (BJA), at year-end 2005, Black inmates represented an estimated 40 percent of all inmates with a sentence of more than one year, while White inmates accounted for 35 percent and Hispanic inmates, 20 percent.[23]

Another researcher, Tyler, focused his study on trust and confidence in police. According to Tyler, trust is divided into two types: institutional and motive based.[24] Three models are used to analyze the two types of trust: crime-control, outcome-based performance, and a process-based policing model. This questionnaire study included a sample of 1,653 New Yorkers: 550 White participants, 455 Black participants, 410 Hispanic participants and 210 other ethnicity participants (twenty-eight respondents declined to give their ethnicity). Variables were operationalized as cooperation with police, institutional trust for the police, motive-based trust for police, fairness of police procedures, race-based judgments, and distributive justice. White respondents expressed higher levels of trust and confidence. The finding also suggests that the public was not completely mistrusting of police, but the public also did not express high levels of trust. White respondents reported the highest levels of cooperation in fighting crime, Blacks the lowest.

Black males sometimes have prejudged all police negatively, which leads them to having aggressive and defensive attitudes when they encounter them. As a result, negative perceptions of police may instigate scenarios that lead to arrests that would not have taken place without the preconceived perceptions.

Although some believe that class has more influence on whether people distrust police, Weitzer and Tuch[25] found that higher educated Blacks are significantly more critical of criminal justice agencies than higher educated Whites. The authors believe that more attention should be given to race and

---

23 Bureau of Justice Statistics. Retrieved from http://www.bjs.gov/.
24 Tom Tyler. "Policing in Black and White: Ethnic Grop Differences in Trust and Confidence in the Police." *Police Quarterly*, 2005: 322–342.
25 Ronald Weitzer and Steven Tuch. "Race, Class and Perceptions of Discrimination of Police." 1999: 494–507.

class when examining people's attitudes toward police. Lundman[26] believes there is a pressing need for additional research on the influences that lead to vehicle searches with one data source being citizen-reported data. Perceptions and understanding of police and laws impact an individual's belief in his or her right to resist arrest. Hemmens and Levin[27] find that the right to resist an unlawful arrest simply allows individuals to act on their own when challenging authority.

The previously referenced research exemplifies the long standing problem and complextities of Black community and police relationships. This research may also aid in providing intervention measures that educate young Black males on what is lawful and what is unlawful, possibly impacting arrests and incarcerations.

African Americans are more likely to have these perceptions of injustice than Whites. Even if police do not engage in "racial profiling" behaviors, minorities may perceive that these forms of discrimination exist.[28] "Debunking the myth of officer friendly" is a quantitative study analyzing minority youths' perceptions toward police. The study took place between the fall of 1993 and 1994.[29] Participants were recruited from three high schools, a boys and girls club, a summer basketball league, and a housing authority summer work program. The study was opened to males age sixteen and seventeen, or three months within the target age. A total of 125 Black males participated in the study, which took place in five towns in a suburban county in central New Jersey. A majority of the Black males reported experiencing the police as a repressive rather than a facilitative agent. The Black males strongly

---

26 Richard Lundman. "Driver Race, Ethnicity, and Gender and Citizen Reports of Vehicle Searches by Police and Search Hits: Toward a Triangulated Scholarly Understanding." *The Journal of Criminal Law And Delinquency*, 2004: 309–345.

27 Craig Hemmens, and Daniel Levin. "Resistance is Futile: The Right to Resist Unlawful Arrest in an Era of Aggressive Policing." *Crime and Delinquency*, 2000: 472–496.

28 Robin Engel. "Citizens' Perceptions of Distributive and Procedural Injustice During Traffic Stops with Police." *Journal of Research in Crime and Delinquency*, 2005: 445–481.

29 Delores D. Jones-Brown. "Debunking the Myth of Officer Friendly." *Journal of Contemporary Criminal Justice*, 2000: 209–229.

believe that race plays a role in police-citizen contacts. There is also concern with the risk of Black males developing negative self-images. Findings suggest that repressive police encounters may reinforce negative attitudes toward police, learned through socialization. This study did not report high levels of delinquency, nor did it report antisocial or delinquent values. This study may also provide data that serves as a foundation for developing in-service training and academic curricula aimed at educating law enforcement officers on why some Black males respond to them in what may be interpreted as negative, defensive, or hostile manners.

And finally, when incarceration rates are estimated separately by age group, Black males in their twenties and thirties are found to have high rates relative to other groups. Expressed in terms of percentages, 8.1 percent of Black males age twenty-five to twenty-nine were in prison on December 31, 2005, compared to 2.6 percent of Hispanic males and about 1.1 percent of White males in the same age group.[30]

SOURCES FOR CURRENT STATISTICS AND RESEARCH

A few years have passed since I first began this project, extending that time period with the publication of the book in a non-dissertation format. With that said, some of the research and statistics are rather old for the academic community. Below you will find resources that allow you to find current statistics and reports. This may assist you in a number of ways. You may find it interesting that a few of the directors of these organizations are African American.

- The Federal Bureau of Investigations-Crime Statistics: https://www.fbi.gov/stats-services/crimestats/
- United States Bureau of Justice Statistics: http://www.bjs.gov/

---

30 Paige M. Harrison and Allen J. Beck. *Bureau of Justice Statistics Bulletin: Prisoners in 2005*. 2006. Http://Www.Ojp.Usdoj.Gov/Bjs/Abstract/P05.Htm (Accessed April 19, 2007).

- US Census Bureau-Criminal Justice Statistics: http://www.census.gov/govs/cj/
- US Department of Justice-Office of Justice Programs: http://ojp.gov/programs/research_stats.htm
- National Criminal Justice Reference Service: https://www.ncjrs.gov/leresources/statistics.html
- Federal Bureau of Prisons: http://www.bop.gov/resources/research_and_reports.jsp
- National Crime Victimization Survey: http://www.bjs.gov/index.cfm?ty=dcdetail&iid=245
- Office of Juvenile Justice and Delinquency Prevention: http://www.ojjdp.gov/

The antagonistic relationship in the United States between Black men and police has existed since the early formative years of this country. Even with the many advances in laws, policies, and professions related to law enforcement and Blacks, the oppressive nature of the relationship still exists in this new millennium. While the church has often been engaged in addressing social justice issues, the focus on spiritual intervention has not systematically been employed to engage Black men with the purpose of intervening in the encounters between young Black males and law enforcement officers. The city of Durham is ideal to select the sample population due to its racial and economic demographics. The Cup of Salvation Deliverance Church's active men's ministry provides an opportunity for a convenient sample population. My childhood, experiences in law enforcement and ministry work bring strength and legitimacy to the overall study.

3

FOUNDATIONS

BIBLICAL FOUNDATIONS

All scripture references are based on the King James Bible. The scriptural foundations selected for this project are Exodus 2:11–15 and Luke 22:47–52:

<u>Exodus 2:11–15</u>

[11] And it came to pass in those days, when Moses was grown, that he went out unto his brethren, and looked on their burdens: and he spied an Egyptian smiting an Hebrew, one of his brethren.

[12] And he looked this way and that way, and when he saw that *there was* no man, he slew the Egyptian, and hid him in the sand.

[13] And when he went out the second day, behold, two men of the Hebrews strove together: and he said to him that did the wrong, Wherefore smitest thou thy fellow?

[14] And he said, Who made thee a prince and a judge over us? Intendest thou to kill me, as thou killedst the Egyptian? And Moses feared, and said, Surely this thing is known.

[15] Now when Pharaoh heard this thing, he sought to slay Moses. But Moses fled from the face of Pharaoh, and dwelt in the land of Midian: and he sat down by a well.

Luke 22:47–52

⁴⁷ And while he yet spake, behold a multitude, and he that was called Judas, one of the twelve, went before them, and drew near unto Jesus to kiss him.
⁴⁸ But Jesus said unto him, Judas, betrayest thou the Son of man with a kiss?
⁴⁹ When they which were about him saw what would follow, they said unto him, Lord, shall we smite with the sword?
⁵⁰ And one of them smote the servant of the high priest, and cut off his right ear.
⁵¹ And Jesus answered and said, Suffer ye thus far. And he touched his ear, and healed him.
⁵² Then Jesus said unto the chief priests, and captains of the temple, and the elders, which were come to him, be ye come out, as against a thief, with swords and staves?

BIBLICAL FOUNDATIONS INTRODUCTION

The Exodus scriptures from the Old Testament were selected due to their deliverance theme. Just as the Hebrew people were enslaved and needed deliverance from their oppressors and oppressive mentality, young Black men need to be delivered from the oppressive arms of the criminal justice system. The deliverance will allow a change in perception, laws, and policies, as well as a change of Black men's negative perception of police and the criminal justice system. Even after the Israelites were delivered, some still had a slavelike and oppressed mentality, not walking in what God had showed them. Young Black men need to be educated so they can engage the criminal justice system and have authority over it, compared to the oppressive "us vs. them" mentality that allows them to be victims of the system. Just as it did not matter that the pharaoh was wrong in his oppression of the Israelites because God had a plan for His chosen people, this study focuses on the deliverance of young Black men from the grips of the criminal justice system and the thinking process that hinders their deliverance, even though they may encounter police who act improperly. Just as Moses was chosen by God to deliver the Hebrews out of Egypt, Christian men can use Christian principles to lead young Black males out of the oppression of the criminal justice system with knowledge and insight.

The synoptic Gospel scriptures (Luke 22:47–52) were selected due to Jesus's control and response when authorities approached and arrested Him on false premises. When the disciples were ready to respond with anger and force toward those doing the arresting, Jesus intervened and recognized that the soldier was only an agent for those in power and was following orders. Jesus even healed the soldier's severed ear to take it a step further, demonstrating that there are options for dealing with unjust people in authority. Jesus did not have a totally passive stance throughout His ministry, calling His disciples to bear arms just prior to His arrest. While Jesus told them to arm themselves, they did not wait for His approval to use the wapons. These scriptures serve as a foundation for this study and suggest there are nonviolent ways to not only resist corrupt and unjust authority members when approached by them, but also to bring about needed change in the US criminal justice system.

OLD TESTAMENT FOUNDATION-EXODUS 2

God had been acting among the people of the world centuries before Christ and the Old Testament provides the historical setting of Christianity, serving as the Bible of Jesus.[31] The Old Testament provides documentation of religious, social, geographical, and political settings.[32] The first translation of the Old Testament was the Greek Septuagint and the English title Exodus has origins in the Greek Septuagint, which means departure or exit.[33] The Septuagint was made for the benefit of Greek-speaking Jews of Alexandria, who could not read Hebrew.

The Old Testament foundation scripture comes from Exodus 2:11–15, as well as the expanded context of Exodus 2. Exodus gives a report of the

---

31 Irving Jensen. *Jensen's Survey of the Old Testament*. Chicago: The Moody Bible Institute of Chicago, 1978, pg. 16.
32 Ibid.,17.
33 Ibid., 25

first of God's deliverances of Israel, which he had promised Abraham. It is the second book of the Pentateuch. Moses is attributed with writing Exodus soon after the completion of the tabernacle as described in Exodus 35–40. When writing Exodus, Moses followed God's instructions and wrote all of the Lord's words (Exodus 24:4).[34] Moses began his leadership of Israel at age eighty and it ended at age 120 (7:7; Deut. 34:7).[35] The exegesis of this passage and other scripture related to leading the oppressed will help to expand and clarify the relationship between Old Testament theology and the twenty-first century philosophy of addressing social justice issues through community engagement.

Chapters 1–10 of Exodus speak of how the daughter of Levi gave birth to a son and tried to hide him to save his life. Pharaoh, who was threatened by an oppressed baby, had ordered all male Hebrew babies to be killed. The baby's mother placed him in an ark made of bulrushes and placed him on the river's bank. The Hebrew slave baby boy was spotted by the pharaoh's daughter and eventually raised in wealth in the pharaoh's house.[36] To what extent do oppressed parents of young Black men believe their son can play a significant role in the world and overcome the social challenges of African Americans? Who speaks that word of success and potential to young Black men? Who speaks to them about how to overcome the oppressive obstacles that may hinder their success and leadership and their ability to deliver other Blacks from today's oppressions such as the criminal justice system? Christian men may serve as the resource and address these questions.

Not all White people are against Black males. Just as the pharaoh's daughter had compassion for a little Hebrew baby, some White officers and criminal justice professionals are interested in helping African American men. If young Black males do not understand this, they may reject some people who have a passion to help them. Christian men can bridge this gap and bring this enlightenment. Do young Black men of today even consider Christian men as

---

34 John MacArthur. *The MacArthur Bible Commentary: Unleasing God's Truth, One Verse at a Time.* Nashville: Thomas Nelson Publishing Co., 2005, pg. 80.
35 Ibid.
36 Ibid.

a source to guide them out of the oppression of the criminal justice system, as the pharaoh's daughter helped Moses? Efforts to provide training and preparation to Christian men so that young Black males consider Christian men as a resource are needed.

God has already chosen those He wants to lead the oppressed and do mighty things for the building of His kingdom. He often prepares them in different ways, sometimes allowing them to experience life's challenges. God has used many Black men who have lived challenging lives, some who have been arrested or imprisoned, just as He used Moses.

VERSE 11

Moses had completed the first forty years of his life in the house and court of the pharaoh, preparing himself for business.[37] Moses boldly owned and espoused the cause of God's people and considered it a better privilege and advantage to be the son of Abraham than to be the son of the pharaoh's daughter.[38]

In this new millennium, there are many African American men who have achieved advances in education, wealth, and political position. Even though Moses had all of the privileges of the pharaoh's house, he still had compassion for his brothers who were being oppressed by his adopted grandfather's laws. There are many African American men who earn salaries and receive numerous benefits because they have been elected to public offices. In these offices, they make, interpret, and enforce the laws. Many of these men profess to be Christians.

Moses had compassion for his brethren who had been left behind to suffer because of oppressive and prejudiced laws, and he went back to their neighborhood to see their burdens. In the new millennium, African American Christian men need to be proactive and go back into the communities where young African American men are struggling with literacy, education, employment,

---

37 Matthew Henry. *Matthew Henry's Commentary on the Whole Bible: Complete and Unabridged in One Volume.* Peabody: Hendrickson Publishers, 2008, pg. 76.
38 Ibid.

crime, and housing to see the extent of their burdens. Moses's compassion for his people and going to where they were is similar to Malcolm X coming from the streets and street people following him because he crystallized and articulated their hurts as he exposed systematic oppression.[39] To lead people who are oppressed, you must have their respect and be able to go where they live. Moses had not gained the respect of his brothers. Christian men must better understand the plight of the Black youth and be willing to go to them, gaining their respect.

Moses killed the Egyptian who was harshly punishing a Hebrew. The Egyptian is believed to have been an Egyptian taskmaster and the Hebrew is believed to have been of the same tribe as Moses and some think he was related to Moses.[40] When Moses killed the Egyptian, it was under God's authority, a special warrant from Heaven.[41] While Moses was chosen by God to fight for and deliver the oppressed, Christian men today answer God's call and say yes to leading the oppressed out of the conditions that victimize them.

Historically, African American males have been victims of oppressive laws and their enforcement. While many of those oppressive laws no longer exist, arrest and incarceration statistics show that African American men are arrested and incarcerated at higher rates than Whites. There is a prejudging attitude toward Black men by some in authority in the criminal justice system, resulting in racist actions. Some African American men also still have the mentality of oppression, thinking that all police officers and the criminal justice system are against them, and therefore, they respond negatively during police encounters. They do not walk in their knowledge and faith that they have the power to change the criminal justice system.

Christian men of all races are called to assist in mentoring and educating young African American men and change their idea that they do not have any power against police and the criminal justice system. Christian men of all

---

39 Carl Ellis, Jr. *Free at Last: The Gospel in the African American Experience.* Downers Grove, IL: Intervarsity Press, 1996, 134.
40 Matthew Henry. *Matthew Henry's Commentary on the Whole Bible: Complete and Unabridged in One Volume.* Peabody: Hendrickson Publishers, 2008, pg. 76.
41 Ibid.

races are also called to challenge and correct any oppressive or improper laws and policies of the criminal justice system. Just as God used Moses to stand up against the oppression of his Hebrew brother, Christian men can stand up for their Christian brothers by educating and mentoring them about law enforcement and criminal justice system relationships, while also seeking to fix a broken criminal justice system.

VERSE 12
Moses believed he was about to do something that would be considered wrong, which is demonstrated by the fact that he looked around to make sure no one was around. He hid the Egyptian he slew in the sand, also demonstrating this fact. Moses felt justified in killing the Egyptian due to the Egyptians' oppressive acts, yet hiding the Egyptian shows Moses had not fully accepted and grown into his calling. This served as a test and perhaps the hesitation demonstrated that his faith was still weak.[42]

VERSE 13
Once again, even though Moses could have stayed in the luxury of his home with the pharaoh, he continued to go out among his brethren, the Hebrews, to check on them. His compassion for his brethren is one of commitment. Christian men, who have achieved what some call success, should especially commit time to going to the neighborhoods where young African American men encounter challenges and could benefit from mentoring about the criminal justice system and police encounters. Christians, especially African American men who have had some versions of success, should be committed to making time to come out of their air conditioned offices and go into communities that can benefit from their presence.

On his second day out, Moses saw two Hebrews fighting and asked why? While it is not clear what they were fighting about, it was unreasonable for

---

42 Ibid.

Hebrews to fight one another, considering they were all oppressed and the Egyptians ruled over them with rigor. The Hebrews that Moses encountered could not comprehend that he was there to assist them out of their oppression. Moses was encouraging them to become friends with each other, just as Christ disapproves of disciples fighting with one another.[43]

Some African American men, especially young men, see a society that is economically unfair and unjust. That is, no matter how hard they work or try, they will not be given the opportunity to achieve economically. Some African American men also feel that the law enforcement and criminal justice systems are racist and Blacks who work for the criminal justice system are against them. These beliefs allow some to justify their illegal activities to gain wealth. They also help justify their opposition when they encounter other Black men who try to guide them out of the clutches of the criminal justice system. Even oppression, at times, does not serve as a catalyst to bring the oppressed together.

Christians will find young African American men fighting one another in gang activity and should believe in the power of the Holy Spirit within them to find the appropriate way to intervene. Gang membership and activities often lead to encounters with the police and have impacted the arrest and incarceration rates of young African American men. In many of these cases, it is not the unjust and oppressive acts of police, but rather the societal conditions, an individual's choice, and laws that are responsible for arrests.

VERSE 14

Moses's first attempt to bring harmony to the two men did not work. One of the two Hebrews fighting challenged Moses and asked him who gave him authority over them? Christian men who go into plighted and oppressed communities should not be surprised if they are met with resistance. They should not be discouraged and continue to press in. As a matter of fact, they should expect rejection and resistance at some level. Often, African

---

43 Luke 9:46; 22:24

American men who have achieved success, and especially those who work for the government, are seen as part of the establishment and those who cannot be trusted, or they are perceived as only being there for self-gratification and they really do not care about what is happening in these underserved communities.

African American men have seen people and programs come and go in their neighborhoods with little commitment and limited impact. The Hebrew challenged Moses for killing the Egyptian who was hurting his fellow Hebrew. This is interesting because even though Moses came to the aid of a Hebrew, another Hebrew was willing to use that against him. This is a mindset that can happen to the oppressed and enslaved; it is a mindset of focusing on self and personal survival. Christian men must understand this same mindset may exist in oppressed and underserved communities today.

Success does not mean a prestigious office or position. Success first means accepting Jesus Christ as your Lord and Savior and realizing hope. It is important for Christian men who still live in oppressed areas and who maybe have not achieved high levels of social economic status to intervene as Moses did. Christian men often have pasts. Maybe they were drug dealers/users, alcoholics, or womanizers. Just as the Hebrew reminded Moses of his actions, those who need the help today may remind Christian men of their pasts. While Moses fled, he did not realize it was part of God's plan for him to be equipped. Christian men who seek to help, educate, and mentor African American men in oppressed communities need to be equipped. If the Hebrews would have accepted Moses for who he was and what he was trying to do as their leader, their deliverance may have started then. Instead, Moses went away for forty years and their deliverance was delayed.

VERSE 15

When the pharaoh heard Moses had slain the Egyptian, he was determined to slay Moses, but Moses ran to a place where he would later be nurtured and developed for a mighty work of God. There are accounts that the pharaoh and his daughter clearly knew that Moses was the son of a Hebrew and should have been killed; Pharaoh spared Moses due to his daughter's affection for him.[44] There are accounts of opportunities for Moses to be killed as requested by Balaam, a wizard of Pharaoh.[45] One perspective that should be considered is how, after many previous opportunities, Pharaoh then decided to arrest and kill Moses. Consider that this may be due to the salient racism hidden in the pharaoh's heart for the Hebrew slave who had become his adopted grandson. Moses had been given all of the rights to the pharaoh's household, but now it was as if that did not matter. Given enough opportunity, his true thoughts of Moses allowed him to seek his death. This may be paralleled with the contemporary issue of laws that restrict racist actions, but there could still be salient racist thoughts in those who enforce the laws, waiting for the opportunity to act against those that their racist beliefs are directed toward. When the Hebrews rejected Moses, God sent him away to Midian.

The Midianites were the descendants of Abraham.[46] They had settled in the Arabian Peninsula along the eastern shore of the Gulf of Aqabah.[47] Moses did not fear the pharaoh because he was timid, but rather because he was cautious.[48] The Hebrew's reaction allowed Moses to see that it was not his time yet and that he should retreat until the time was right. Young Black men must be taught when to fight back and when the environment is appropriate for that. Not responding aggressively to police officers' illegal actions is not a sign of weakness or cowardice. Rather the men should address the injustice in the appropriate forum.

In today's society, not everyone will be happy with empowering the oppressed. This was exemplified with Reverend Dr. Martin King, Jr. Christian men are needed to empower and equip oppressed African American men. Not everyone will be happy with the rise of and strengthening of African American men. The potential influence in voting, economics, and addressing social justice issues has great potential for changing local communities, and

---

44 Kirsch, Johnathan. *Moses: A Life*. New York: Ballantine Books, 1998, 61.
45 Ibid.
46 Gen 25:1–4.
47 John MacArthur. *The MacArthur Bible Commentary: Unleasing God's Truth, One Verse at a Time*. Nashville: Thomas Nelson Publishing Co., 2005.
48 Ibid.

therefore the nation. There will be those who will see this as a threat to their power and success. This is why men who seek to bring African American men to an awakening era must be in tune with the Holy Spirit in them and provided with the appropriate training and education that will prepare them for success.

NEW TESTAMENT FOUNDATION-LUKE 22

The New Testament Foundation scripture comes from Luke 22:47–52. Luke is acknowledged as the longest book of the New Testament and it gives the most comprehensive account of the life of Christ and emphasizes the "exact" truth and "consecutive order."[49] While the author of Luke is not named, evidence strongly supports that it is Luke and that it was written around AD 60.[50] All biblical survey and analytical study of text should involve content (what the Bible says) and form (how it says it). According to Jensen, Luke uses the content of exact truth and the form of consecutive orderliness. Luke had Greek parents and this heritage most likely made him the only Gentile writer of the New Testament. The humanity of Jesus is exemplified through the large number of prayers throughout the book of Luke, with eleven of the fifteen occasions of Christ praying in the Gospels taking place in Luke.[51]

It is important to note that Judas's identification of Jesus and the arrest and violence were acts of Satan. Baffled in his attempts to bring fear to Jesus, he turns to force and arms and brings a party into the field to seize him, and Satan was *in them.*[52] Satan will use the negative relationships between Black men and police to keep Black men oppressed and imprisoned.

The selected scripture is preceded by Jesus correcting the disciples for sleeping "on the job." When Jesus went to the Mount of Olives to pray, he

---

[49] Irving Jensen. *Jensen's Survey of the New Testament.* Chicago: The Moody Bible Institute of Chicago, 1981.
[50] Ibid.
[51] Ibid.
[52] Ibid.

told the disciples to pray so they would not fall into temptation. Jesus was not far away as he prayed to God to strengthen him. God granted his request and sent an angel. When Jesus returned to the disciples, he found them asleep. He commanded them to get up before they fall into temptation. This parallels the new millennium Christians in that many are sleeping on the job. That is, they are not going into the areas of the oppressed and poor to assist them. Many Christians create superficial programs that do not have long-term systemic impact. While Christians give food and clothing, statistics showing high poverty and dropout rates demonstrate that the oppressed and poor are not shown how to come out of poverty and oppression, and the government is not being changed from a system that keeps the oppressed oppressed and the poor poor.

The arrest rates and incarceration rates of African American men have continued to be much higher compared to White men decades later. Jesus calls for the disciples to pray so they may not fall into temptation. Specific measures must be taken today to have Christians focus on prayer that will strengthen them so they will not fall into the temptation of sleepiness toward the issues beyond the walls of the church. African American men fall behind in literacy, education, and economics, influencing the rates of arrests and incarcerations. It is as if Christian men were sleeping in the church in the new millennium.

When studying the selected New Testament scriptures and their foundation for this project, one must have an understanding of the complex relationship between Jesus and the authority of Rome. This relationship was complicated even more by the relationships among those of Jewish authority, Roman authority, and Jesus. Several theologians provide insight into these relationships.

JESUS AND ROMAN AUTHORITY

Howard Thurman provides an analysis of Roman and Jewish relationships and the atmosphere that characterized life in a Jewish community when Jesus was a youth in Palestine. According to Thurman, "In essence, Rome was the enemy; Rome symbolized total frustration; Rome was the great barrier to peace of mind. And Rome was everywhere."[53] This atmosphere parallels the present-day atmosphere in which the police symbolize total frustration for some young Black men. They challenge their peace of mind, and the police are everywhere.

Howard goes on to explain the psychological climate in which Jesus began his teaching ministry. He explains that Israel was a minority in the Greco-Roman world and was hurting under the loss of status, freedom, and autonomy, haunted by a dream of restoration of a lost glory and former greatness.[54] This psychological climate is similar to the climate of Black men in America today. It is important to have an understanding of the history of the Roman Empire during the time of the selected scripture.

John McRay chronicles the history of the Roman Empire in the *Holman Illustrated Bible*.[55] According to McRay, the Roman Empire was born after the fall of the Republic of Rome government around 27 BC. While the reasons for the fall of the Republic of Rome are complicated and not fully clear, some of the reasons include unrest among the classes, problems in maintaining order, and difficulty recruiting soldiers. Julius Caesar stepped in declaring himself as dictator in 44 BC after a vacuum of leadership in the Republic of Rome, but his dictatorship style provoked a group of senatorial assassins to assassinate him on the Ides of March. After a series of power-sharing moves, Octavian eventually became the sole ruler, taking the name Augustus Caesar, and becoming the first emperor of Rome in 27 BC. Augusts went on to establish extensive programs of social, religious, and moral reform. Traditional religion was stressed with 82 pagan temples renovated. Jesus Christ was born during the reign of Augustus, which occurred from 27 BC to A.D. 14. Without question, Roman rule was oppressive: "Everything about Roman occupation was hateful to the Jews, from oppressive taxes to physical abuse by Roman soldiers to the repugnant idea that the Roman leader was a god."[56]

---

53 Howard Thurman. *Jesus and the Disinherited*. Boston: Beacon Press, 1996, 12.
54 Ibid, 22.
55 John McRay. "How the Jews Lived in Jesus' Time." 2003. http://ancienthistory.about.com/od/biblicalhistory/a/How-the-Jews-Lived-in-Jesus-Time.htm.
56 Ibid,1415.

Terry Dashner provides an overview of Jesus and his views toward government. In "Jesus' Views of Civil Government,"[57] Terry Dashner provides insight on just that. Considering law enforcement officers are agents of the government, it is important to take a look at how Jesus responded to government during his time. The Roman authority was the government that was in place while Jesus walked the earth, and He demonstrates how to relate to the Roman government throughout the New Testament. While Jesus addressed issues of an unjust government, he made statements throughout the New Testament supporting civil government.[58] Jesus advised tax collectors to continue their work, but to be just and fair. Jesus advised the Roman centurions, military law enforcement of the time, that they should not use their position of authority and power as a way of extorting favor from those under their rule. Both tax collectors and centurions were legitimate occupations for maintaining a civil government.

Today, many would agree that law enforcement and the criminal justice system are legitimate occupations and necessary. The issue is making sure policies and actions are not racist or oppressive. African American men must be educated on how to influence and change the criminal justice system at the local level. It is acceptable for Black men to aggressively take a stance against inappropriate actions, laws, and policies at the hands of law enforcement, but they must be taught the appropriate measures and methods to do so.

Jesus did not rebuke Peter for carrying the sword he used to strike the servant of the high priest; he had actually told him to carry the sword. Jesus rebuked Peter for using the sword unlawfully. Dashner does well at differentiating between civil government and those who work in it when he states, "Men who fill positions of civil government may be evil, but the civil government as a whole is not evil, but sanctioned by God Almighty to keep and maintain lawful order in society."[59] Christian men should seek to put just men in positions of authority. Christian men should seek to recruit young Black males to

---

57 Terry Dashner. "Jesus' Views on Civil Government." Broken Arrow: GoArticles.com, October 5, 2005.
58 Ibid., 1.
59 Ibid., 2.

become law enforcement officers, correctional officers, district attorneys, and judges. Barry Benning provides another view of Jesus and Roman authority.

Barry Benning researched the relationship between Jesus and Romans of authority in *Roman Influence on the Birth of Christianity*.[60] While I do not agree with some of his critical perspectives on Jesus's experiences, Benning provides documented perspectives that bring insight into how Jesus viewed Roman authority. Benning not only addresses Roman authority during the time of Christ, but also identifies the established Jewish religious order as a dominating authority. A major portion of his work focuses on the conflict between Roman authority and Jewish authority. As the recognized and formal civil authority, it was not unusual for Roman authority to meddle in the affairs of the Jewish people.

The primary point is that it is well documented that the teachings of Jesus were very different from the teachings of Judaism. Jesus addressed Roman authority, as well as the Jewish doctrine and authority of His time. It is interesting to note that Jesus was often critical of Jewish order, such as offering support and public praise of a Roman centurion. Jesus often encouraged submissive behavior to those who oppress, *But if any one strikes you on the right cheek, turn to him the other also,*[61] *Love your enemies and pray for those who persecute you,*[62] *Blessed are the meek, the poor, the peacemakers.*[63] These Christian teachings are in contrast to the nature of Jewish people of that time, who were proud and priestly. Christianity is very clear about the expectations of those in power: John states that the tax collector should accept only the appointed amount[64] and soldiers must not rob anyone by violence or false accusation and should be content with their wages.[65]

The overarching points for the new millennium when addressing Black males and police are: Christian principles should be adopted to address the

---

60 Barry Benning. http://www.barrybenning.com/roman_influence.pdf., n.d., pg. 5.
61 Matthew 5:39.
62 Matthew 5:44.
63 Matthew 5:3–10.
64 Luke 3:13
65 Luke 3:14

oppressive nature of the criminal justice system; laws, policies, and practices of the criminal justice system should be addressed; young Black males should not respond aggressively to inappropriate actions of law enforcement, but address the inappropriate and illegal issues immediately following the incidents.

In *The Politics of Jesus*, Obery Hendricks, Jr. makes it clear that the basis of *mishpat*, the biblical concept of justice, oppression, and exploitation, have no rightful place in God's plan for humanity, and that *malkuth shamayim*, the unquestioned conviction that only God has the right to rule, as was taught throughout biblical Israel's existence, are guiding forces even today.[66]

The following scriptures were selected because they teach that Christian men must focus on the root of the problem and not be distracted by emotions of anger against those who are only agents for the government and in control. Luke shows how Christian men can be aggressive in pursuit of change, yet not violent.

VERSE 47

The selected scripture begins while Jesus is speaking to the disciples about praying to overcome temptation rather than sleeping. A crowd approaches, led by Judas, one of the disciples. The crowd includes authorities who are carrying out a plot to arrest Jesus, and Judas has agreed to identify his leader for money. The heavily armed representatives were of the Sanhedrin.[67] Romans with lanterns, torches, and weapons accompanied them.[68] There are those in the church today who are there for their own personal gain, just like Judas. Rather than doing the work of God, they are more interested in self-glorification and getting paid. Unfortunately, some of these Christians are pastors and leaders of churches. They have turned on God for their own benefit. Since slavery and during the Civil Rights era, there have been and continue to be Christian leaders who are more interested in keeping the peace and serving as a voice for the government and economic powers that are doing the oppressing.

---

66 Obery Hendricks. *The Politics of Jesus*. Garden City: Doubleday, 2006, p. 94.
67 Matt. 26:47; Mark 14:43.
68 John 18:3.

VERSE 48

Jesus asks Judas very directly and specifically if he is betraying him with a kiss. Jesus wants Judas to know HE knows why he's betraying Him with a kiss. Judas uses a symbol of love and respect to betray Jesus. Just as Jesus was aware of Judas's heart and actions, God is aware of those who use His name and His Church for self-glorification and preservation rather than kingdom-building and addressing the needs of the poor and oppressed.

VERSE 49

Jesus previously instructed the disciples to take up swords because they were about to enter a different phase. When they were ready to arm all who would accompany Him, Jesus told them that only a couple of swords were needed. Due to this, compared to other journeys, the disciples were armed according to Jesus's direction. Jesus was letting them know that times were changing and some defense may be necessary. During today's era, Jesus does not expect disciples to go into dangerous areas blindly. Christians of the new millennium must be aware that violence and protection may be necessary, but limited and controlled.

VERSE 50

Rather quickly, a disciple, believed by some to be Peter, struck one of the high priest's servants (believed to be Malchus), cutting off his right ear. Only the Book of John says that the swordsman was Peter and the victim was named Malchus.[69] Some believe that Peter intended to cut off the guard's head and missed, cutting off his ear. Simon/Peter was a zealot and the zealots were fanatical nationalists, sworn to assassinate every traitor and every Roman they could.[70] A zealot was a militaristic patriotic party in Judaism. This party was determined to free the land of foreign control by whatever means necessary.[71]

---

69 John 18:10.
70 William Barclay. *The Gospel of Luke*. Louisville, KY: Westminster Press, 1975, 75.
71 Donald J. Selby. *Introduction to the New Testament: The Word Became Flesh*. Wichita: Macmillan Publishing, 1971, 488.

This may have influenced his quick and violent reaction, even after following Jesus. The disciples asked Jesus if they should strike with their swords, but they were so emotional, they did not even wait to hear his response. What would have been Jesus's response?

Christians today need continued training in how to approach representatives of the government, similar to the training that took place during the Civil Rights Era.[72] The high priest's servant was following his boss's directions. Christian men must begin to teach young Black men that the police are paid servants of the government, often following the laws that have been put in place. This is not to say that some officers are not abusive and corrupt. Today most encounters with police are not abusive. This will be difficult for some to accept. There is a system in place to address improper arrests and citations. There is a larger system in place to address inappropriate laws and those who make the laws. There is yet another system in place that allows for organized civil disobedience.

VERSE 51

Jesus responded to the violent act of cutting off the ear with the command, "No more of this!" Jesus made it absolutely clear that violence of this measure was not appropriate. There is no need to physically assault those who are carrying out the duties of the criminal justice system. Jesus healed the ear of the guard who had been attacked. This is the only time that Jesus healed someone without being asked to do it, and healed someone who did not proclaim Him afterward. Jesus had compassion for the guard who was carrying out a duty, and who could be considered his enemy, yet his miracle and compassion did not appear to have any impact on the men. John 18:6 records the explosive power of Jesus's words knocking the men to the ground and this also appeared to have limited impact on them to stop the arrest. Jesus had the power to strike the guards down, but brings them no harm. Christian men must be instructed on how to educate and mentor young African American

---

72 John Lewis, Andrew Aydin, and Nate Powell. *March: Book One*. N.D.

men on how to respond to law enforcement encounters. They do not have to accept illegal and improper activity, but rather address it with the appropriate authority.

VERSE 52

Jesus asks the officials who came to arrest him if the crowd, force, and weaponry were necessary. Jesus reminded them that their show of force and methods were excessive. Some police officers respond to young African American males with aggressiveness out of fear. Those who arrested Jesus were following the orders of the chief priests and captains of the temple. Without question, law enforcement must have an appropriate selection of officers, training, and discipline. African American males must understand that not all law enforcement officers are the same and they will have different attitudes and perceptions of African American men. Some fear them, some are prejudiced, some understand them, and some have compassion for them. Just as Jesus knew those who came to arrest him, African American men must better understand the law enforcement officers they may encounter and the most effective way to respond to them. While the history between Black men and police has been antagonistic, there are common benefits for collaboration and mutual respect. This is exemplified in the work of Howard Thurman.

In the *Search for Common Ground,* Thurman discusses the search for a common consciousness.[73] As an example of how two seemingly opposing forces can find common ground and peace, he tells a story of little girl playing with a rattlesnake. He witnesses an infant girl playing with a rattlesnake in the yard of one of his friends. The friend's father made sure that Thurman did not interfere with the potentially deadly situation. The baby girl was playing with the rattlesnake, turning it over on its back as the snake crawled back and forth around her. It was very clear that they were playing with each other. It was also important that no one interrupted the harmony with disharmony created by noise or sudden movement. When the baby grew tired of playing with the

---

73 Howard Thurman. *The Search for Common Ground.* Friends United Press, 1986, 57.

deadly snake, the baby started crawling toward the steps. At this point, the snake turned and slithered toward the woods. The father of the friend and baby girl killed the snake with a shotgun. It was as if two different expressions of life, normally antagonistic to each, had dropped back into some common ground and there reestablished a sense of harmony through which they were relating to each other at a conscious level.

While the relationship between Black men and law enforcement in America has been historically antagonistic, there is a common ground to be found and shared that benefits society and the community as a whole. There is that potential for crime in the Black community to decrease, for injuries to Black men to decline, and for the number of arrests of Black males to be reduced. Just as it took Jesus to bring Matthew, a tax collector, together with Peter, a zealot, to carry on His Word as disciples, it will take Christ using diverse Christian men together to strengthen the relationship between Black men and police.[74]

THEOLOGICAL FOUNDATION: PRACTICAL THEOLOGY

The theological foundation frames the overarching approach and purpose of this research project through the lens of the study of God. Practical theology was selected to serve as the theological foundation of the contemporary problem, which is how to strengthen the relationships between police and the Black community in the new millennium. According to Veling, "Practical theology, as its name suggests, is less a thing to be defined as it is an activity to be done."[75] Veling continues to state, "...it is only in the practice or doing of theology that we begin to realize and understand its meanings and its workings more deeply."[76]

Just as it took God to deliver Israel from the hands of her oppressors and it takes God to deliver the unsaved from sin and hell, I believe it will

---

74 William Barclay. *The Gospel of Luke*. Louisville, KY: Westminster Press, 1975, 75.
75 Terry Veling. *Practical Theology: On Earth as It Is in Heaven*. Maryknoll, NY: Orbis Books, 2005, 4.
76 Ibid.

take God, using the church, to deliver African American Black men from the historical hands of an oppressive criminal justice system in the United States. Acts 10:38 states, "How God anointed Jesus of Nazareth with the Holy Ghost and with power: who went about doing good, and healing all that were oppressed of the devil; for God was with him."[77] Men of the church today must know they have the anointing of the Holy Spirit and are equipped to fix what has not been resolved for decades. Since the early formative years of the United States and the usage of slave police to catch men who fled their masters, law enforcement and African American men have had an adversarial relationship.

Practical theology can provide an understanding of how faith and an intimate relationship with God can guide the action in this now contemporary circumstance, while providing the rationale for church involvement. According to Anderson:

> Practical theology is a dynamic process of reflective, critical inquiry into the praxis of the church in the world and God's purposes for humanity, carried out in the light of Christian scripture and tradition, and in critical dialogue with other sources of knowledge. As a theological discipline, its primary purpose is to ensure that the church's public proclamation and praxis in the world faithfully reflect the nature and purpose of God's continuing mission to the world and in so doing *authentically* addresses the *contemporary context* into which the church seeks to minister.[78]

For the purposes of this study, faith can guide Christian men in understanding how to strengthen the relationship between young Black men and police from a Christlike perspective, knowing things will be changed. Christian men must first come to believe that they are the vessel God will use to remedy the historical problem, believing that God is in control.

---

77 Acts 10:38.
78 Ray Anderson. *The Shape of Practical Theology: Empowering Ministry With Theological Praxis*. Downers Grove, IL: InterVarsity Press, 2001, 22.

According to Osmer, practical theology is the practical application of theology to everyday life.[79] The four key questions and tasks in practical theology are:

1. What is going on?
2. Why is this going on?
3. What ought to be going on?
4. How might we respond?

Answering these questions as a frame for this project, the responses are as follows:

1. What is going on within the church to address the issue of the relationship between Black males and police?
2. Why is the church taking the approach that it takes—if any—to strengthen the relationship between Black men and the police and to change policies/practices within the criminal justice system?
3. What should the church do to strengthen the relationship between Black men and the police?
4. How might the church respond to aggressive police action toward Black men and the disproportionate number of Black men in the criminal justice system today?

Political theology or public theology are often associated with practical theology and are seen as a branch of political philosophy, which investigates the ways in which theological concepts or ways of thinking underlie political, social, economic, and cultural discourses.[80]

It is important to understand that practical theology in the new millennium is more than applying theological concepts to a social situation, and that

---

79 Richard R. Osmer. *Practical Theology: An Introduction*. William B. Eerdmans Publishing Co., 2008.
80 John Bowker. "Political theology." *The Concise Oxford Dictionary of World Religions*. 1997. *Encyclopedia.com*. (November 9, 2014). http://www.encyclopedia.com/doc/1O101-Politicaltheology.html.

theology should be transformed by the conditions that people of faith must utilize as they participate in shaping the future. Practical theology, as well as all theology, should be adapted to the social conditions of the time. One example of this is demonstrated by looking at the social phenomenon of the relationship between police and Black males during different eras. Under the practical theological lens, Christians may have addressed the issue differently during the Jim Crow era compared to the new millennium era, in which the rights and authority of Blacks have advanced.

Theology can be divided into two paradigms. First, the paradigm of theology is comprised of a set of subdisciplines. Second, all of theology is practical.[81] In the first paradigm, practical theology is a subdiscipline of theology. In the second paradigm, the primary purpose of all theology is to have a practical end or purpose. In addition to being divided into two paradigms, theology can be divided into four categories: theology as the knowledge of God, theology as science, theology as a discipline of study, and theology as systemic (a more modern use of theology).[82] The manner in which people study God has grown as society has grown, and it has become more complex. While the manner in which we study God has evolved, His Word has remained the same. Practical theology has undergone changes and developments as the study of God has developed.

According to Hazle, practical theology has undergone a "rebirth" over the last three decades. First, it has been concerned with equipping people for tasks such as preaching and pastoral care. Second, that rebirth has challenged the traditional methodologies of theological synthesis, developing socio-theological perspectives like political theology.[83] While many things stay the same, there is no question that society has changed, and the theological synthesis has become more complex. As an example, three decades ago, computers and the Internet did not offer the technological advancements available today.

---

81 Dave Hazle. "Practical Theology Today and the Implications for Mission." *International Review of Mission* 92, no. 366 (2003): 345. https://www.questia.com/read/1G1-107761086/practical-theology-today-and-the-implications-for, pg. 1.
82 Ibid, 4.
83 Ibid, 2.

Computers were expensive and Internet access was not mobile as it is today. Just as there are many positive advances, Satan takes advantage of opportunities as well through social ills like pornography and child exploitation. These Internet advances can also provide Christians Bible study and daily devotional models

Social media serves as an outlet for Christians to collectively share the Word of God. It is not unusual to discover a number of Christian blogs on the Internet. What impact have these technological advances had on the study of the nature of God and religious truth? How should Christians approach and receive these advanced technologies and others according to the Word of God? The criminal justice system has greatly expanded in many areas over the past several decades as well, yet Black men are still disproportionally represented in the criminal justice system. In addition, Blacks have a more negative perception of police than Whites. Both of these social phenomena continue to exist, even though there have been many Blacks who have entered the criminal justice profession, reaching high levels of authority and position. Practical theology is an appropriate means for exploring and addressing these social phenomena, giving the church a reason to get involved in social policies that oppress. While considered a young theological perspective, practical theology is not new.

Practical theology has a rich and long history, dating back to the Enlightenment, when the German theologian Friedrich Schleiermacher was faced with the threat of expulsion from the university setting for proposing that theology was essentially practical, like law and medicine. Schleiermacher's proposal laid the foundation for practical theology as an applied theology.[84]

While in graduate school at the University of Tennessee, studying sociology and criminology, I struggled with synthesizing some aspects of sociological theory. A professor and mentor seeking to help with the problem then asked if I believed in studying theory for the purpose of understanding it, or if I believed in studying theory to address issues in society. Quickly I responded, "Why would someone study sociological theory just for the purpose of

---

84 Ibid, 4.

understanding theory?" The professor replied, "I understand your challenge with some of the perspectives that some professors teach." She went on to say something along the lines that I come from a relatively new paradigm of social theory called applied sociology and not everyone views and studies sociological theory from that perspective.

My challenge was that my Master of Public Administration degree emphasized practice management principles and organizational theories rather than sociological theories. With more than twenty years in law enforcement, reaching the rank of police chief, I had developed a perspective that one only studied criminological theory to better understand and find solutions for crime and societal problems. This perspective is complementary to Hazle's second paradigm that the primary purpose of all theology is to address problems of the world from a Godly and spiritual approach and one would not study theology with a focus only on what happens in the church's epistemological approach.

From this perspective, practical theology is most appropriate from an applied perspective to frame and address the historical and critical social phenomenon of the negative and often hostile relationship between African American men and police, going back to the role of slave police. It will take the Spirit of Christ to remedy what politicians, activists, sociologists, and bureaucrats have not been able to remedy for centuries. Romans 13:4 states, "For he is the minister of God to thee for good. But if thou do that which is evil, be afraid; for he beareth not the sword in vain: for he is the minister of God, a revenger to [execute] wrath upon him that doeth evil."[85] Black men must be reminded not to respond violently in the street to aggressive police action, knowing that God will handle those who oppress and do evil.

From a practical and applied theological approach, one can find what God would have us do to remedy the historical and often oppressive relationship between Black men and police in the United States. While many have sought solutions from an activist, political, and sociological perspective, few have sought a Christian perspective. Government has engaged the church, but

---

85 Rom 13:4.

the church has not led the way. It is as if the church augmented government activities, rather than government augmenting church mission.

Theology should provide an understanding of how to address contemporary problems through seeking an understanding of God and Christ from a mission approach. Theology is missological, that is, according to Hazle, "It is the concern for appropriate mission that drives theological reflections and effective mission in the service of the gospel, and that ultimately judges the appropriateness of theological understanding."[86]

From this mission approach, going out beyond the walls of the church, theology should respond to community specifics, seeking a more in-depth understanding of contextual realities. According to Andrews, "Leaders in the New Testament were often found right at the point of engagement in ministry. Leaders equip people for ministry by modeling, actively teaching, casting vision, and identifying opportunities."[87] For the purpose of this project, one must seek a deeper understanding of the historically oppressive relationship between Black men and the police, the generational exchange of views of police, violent police activity, media, peer association, prison race statistics, poverty, etc., to address this issue. Hazle states:

> "A church that bases its theology on a practical paradigm understands that its mission must arise out of its deepening awareness of its context, and therefore invest in the analysis of the context."[88]

A mission view is engaged out of response to the understanding of God's intention and is built on sources rooted in Christian faith, like scriptures and traditions. From a practical theological approach, the church takes a mission view of addressing the relationship between Black males and police in

---

86 Dave Hazle. "Practical Theology Today and the Implications for Mission." *International Review of Mission* 92, no. 366 (2003): 345. https://www.questia.com/read/1G1-107761086/practical-theology-today-and-the-implications-for, 5.
87 Alan Andrews. *The Kingdom Life: A Practical Theology of Discipleship and Spiritual Formation,* Colorado Springs, CO: NavaPress, 2010, 310.
88 Ibid., 10.

their local community, using Christian principles and prayer for direction. In addressing the social conditions of the community, the church must use the multidisciplinary approach and scientific research advocated by practical theology to better understand community contexts of race, crime, economics, and poverty, when seeking God's word on solutions, and acknowledging that community contexts change over time.

The Public Influences of African American Churches Project (PIAAC) exemplifies Black church and policy engagement from a practical theological approach. PIAAC is based at the Leadership Center at Morehouse College and chronicled in *Long March Ahead: African American Churches and Public Policy in Post-Civil Rights America*.[89] This edited book is the second volume of two and both volumes provide analysis of data received from surveying 1,956 black churches, located in nineteen major cities throughout the nation and twenty-six small rural counties in the south. The goal of the project was to fill the gap in scholarly research related to Black church involvement in the political arena that goes beyond activism.[90] The primary difference between engagement via political theology and activism is the seeking of the Word of God for direction and purpose. African American church involvement in law enforcement social policy is not new, as demonstrated in the collaboration with police in Boston.

In *Long March Ahead; African American Churches and Public Policy in Post-Civil Rights America*, Christopher Winship authored the essay, *End of a Miracle? Crime, Faith, and Partnership in Boston in the 1990s.*[91] The Boston Miracle refers to the dramatic drop in crime in Boston during the 1990s. Homicides decreased from 152 in 1990 to 31 in 1999, with most of the drop occurring for individuals under the age of twenty-four. For that age group, the number of crimes they committed decreased from 73 in 1990 to

---

89 Drew Smith. *Long March Ahead: African American Churches and Public Policy in Post-Civil Rights America*. Durham: Duke University Press, 2004.

90 Ibid, ix.

91 Christopher Winship. "End of a Miracle? Crime, Faith, and Partnership in Boston in the 1990s." In *Long March Ahead*, by R. Drew Smith, 171–192. Durham and London: Duke University Press, 2004.

15 in 1999. One of the amazing statistics is that no teenagers were killed during a twenty-nine month period ending in January, 1998. This is the *Boston Miracle*.[92]

Some give credit to the decline in violence to a partnership between police and inner city Black ministers, which was called the Ten Point Coalition. Its focus was on youth violence. *Newsweek* (June 1, 1998), featured the Ten Point Coalition and how the Black ministers came to work with police to address the problem of gangs and youth violence.[93] As a former police chief, I know there are many variables that may contribute to a decline or increase in crime, but the partnership between Black ministers and police may be considered a miracle in itself, considering the negative history between the Black community and police in Boston. Knowingly or not, the ministers used an approach framed by practical theology. Their partnership extended beyond activism. They played an integral role in framing public policy.

The end of the 1990s could have been different if it were not for the collaboration. Boston had experienced a number of incidents that had the possibility of leading to rioting and aggressive actions toward Black males by police, similar to other cities and communities. In March of 1994, a retired Black minister died from a heart attack when police broke into the wrong apartment during a drug raid. In 1995, a Black undercover officer was beaten by a racially mixed group of officers after being mistaken as a fleeing suspect. Also in 1995, a Black gang member shot and killed an assistant district attorney as he sat in his car on his way home from work.[94]

The Ten Point Coalition also assisted in bringing resolution to critical policy issues that had the potential of negatively impacting the Black community. These issues involved the Boston City Hospital and the school board. Boston had a reputation for racist and oppressive public policy, yet critical issues in the 1970s and 1980s were defined and debated from a racial perspective and

---

92 Ibid, 171.
93 Ibid.
94 Ibid., 174.

the collaboration among Black ministers, police, and city government ushered in a new era of addressing public policy.[95]

As with many police departments, Boston also faced the reality of the need to address policies and practices within the police department. Boston PD faced many issues related to a lack of professionalism, "good ol' boy" hiring/promoting, and a lack of concern for change and improvement. A commission was established to investigate the police department after a $1 million wrongful death lawsuit. Through Black ministers willing to work beyond the walls of their church to address community problems, Boston was able to work with police and other government entities to improve not only police relations, but also other public sector organizations.[96]

The Ten Point Coalition demonstrates that Black churches have successfully collaborated with police to address social and political policy issues at critical times. The collaboration had greater impact than addressing the issues of youth violence; it allowed police and Black males to gain a better understanding of one another. This is just one example of political theology that this research project seeks to build upon.

This study seeks to equip men in the church to help young Black males improve their views of police using a foundation of practical theology. Practical theology has grown over the years. A basic Internet search shows a number of practical theology programs at higher education institutions that are committed to research and study, as well as a number of organizations dedicated to the theological perspective. The Association of Practical Theology (APT) lists the following universities with doctoral programs in the field of study:[97]

1. Boston University School of Theology
2. Claremont School of Theology
3. Emory University
4. Garrett-Evangelical Theological Seminary

---

95 Ibid., 175.
96 Ibid.
97 The Association of Practical Theology. Retrieved from http://practicaltheology.org/ on November 5, 2014.

5. St. Thomas University
6. Princeton Theological Seminary
7. Vanderbilt University

According to the APT website, the purpose of the association is to promote critical discourse that integrates theological reflection and practice:

> Practical Theology focuses on the needs and questions of today's people. Theological answers of the past are not necessarily fitted for the future of the Christian religion because of the change in modern society. How can one understand the biblical wonder-stories in a time in which modern sciences deepen our insight into the laws of nature? How can people who want to decide autonomously on the basis of arguments, give authority to the bible as the Word of God and to the Church? How can modern people pray to God, and to which God? Practical theology as a science of the crises of the Christian religion in modern society has an intrinsic relation to hermeneutics.[98]

The purpose statement provided by the APT website provides an appropriate summary and view of practical theology. Practical theology can provide an understanding of how faith and an intimate relationship with God can guide action in contemporary circumstances, while providing rationale for church involvement. African American church involvement in law enforcement and social policy is not new, as demonstrated in the collaboration with police in Boston. Romans 13:1 states, "Let every soul be subject unto the higher powers. For there is no power but of God: the powers that be are ordained of God."[99] Christian men must be reminded that it is God who is in control.

---

98 Chris Hermans and Mary Elizabeth Moore, "Chapter One: The Contribution of Empirical Theology by Johannes A. Van Der Ven: An Introduction," in *Hermeneutics and Empirical Research in Practical Theology: The Contribution of Empirical Theology by Johannes A. Van Der Ven*, ed. Chris A.M. Hermans and Mary E. Moore (Boston: Brill, 2004), 3, https://www.questia.com/read/117547298.

99 Romans 13:1.

He even controls law enforcement, and His concepts should be followed to address the oppressive actions of government officials.

Practical theology challenges and mandates the church to become engaged in social justice issues within the community in order help bring resolution. Nelson Mandela stressed the importance of educated church leadership engaging the community when he stated, "I learned from Gaur that a degree was not in itself a guarantee of leadership and that it meant nothing unless one went out into the community to prove oneself."[100] Gaur Radebe was an activist in both the Communist Party of South Africa and the African National Congress.

HISTORICAL/CONTEMPORARY FOUNDATIONS

THE CHURCH AND SOCIAL JUSTICE
Jesus and the Disinherited: Thurman Howard
The forward of *Jesus and the Disinherited* was written by Vincent Harding and begins with sharing the differences between Howard's work and liberation theology.[101] Harding challenges the reader not to prejudge the focus of *Jesus and the Disinherited* by assuming it follows the 1940 version of liberation theology and the message that God is on the side of the oppressed with powerful condemnation of the oppressors and cruel systems of dehumanization. Harding then goes on to say that Howard's work "…can be more accurately described as a profound quest for a liberating spirituality, a way of exploring and experiencing those crucial life points where personal and societal transformation are creatively joined."

This study is based on a premise that improving the relationships between Black males and police in the United States will take a transformation of Christian men. Christian men must see the solution from a spiritual mind, rather than a carnal mind. Howard possessed an intimate understanding of

---

100 Nelson Mandela. *Long Walk to Freedom: The Autobiography of Nelson Mandela.* Boston: Back Bay Books, 1995. 64.
101 Thurman, Howard. *Jesus and the Disinherited.* Boston: Beacon Press, 1996, vii.

the harsh conditions of oppression that existed in the United States and had an appreciation for the people who took a stance against the harshness without losing their own humanity or betraying their own souls.[102] Christian men must stand up against the harsh and, at times oppressive, criminal justice system without allowing Satan to lead them to abandoning their relationship with Christ and the principles He teaches. As a police chief, community activist, college professor, and minister of the Gospel, I have witnessed many Black men who have a high level of hate and anger toward police. Howard has dedicated a chapter of his book to the topic of hate.

Howard believes that Christianity has been reluctant to examine hatred and has been rather sentimental in its attempts to address hatred in human life. According to Howard, hatred cannot be defined, but it can be described, and he provides four progressive elements of description.

1. Hatred often begins in a situation in which there is contact without fellowship, contact that is devoid of any of the primary overtures of warmth and fellow-feeling and genuineness.
2. Contacts without fellowship tend to express themselves in the kind of understanding that is strikingly unsympathetic.
3. An unsympathetic understanding tends to express itself in the active functioning of ill will.
4. Ill will, when dramatized in a human being, becomes hatred walking on earth.[103]

Rather than using this model only toward the attitude of the strong to the weak, or the oppressor to the oppressed, it can be used to synthesize the attitude of the oppressed toward the oppressor, or for the sake of this study, Black men toward Police. According to Howard, "Hatred, in the mind and spirit of the disinherited, is born out of great bitterness—a bitterness that is made possible by sustained resentment which is bottled up until it distills an

---

102 Ibid, ix.
103 Ibid, 69.

essence of vitality, giving to the individual in who this is happening a radical and fundamental basis for self-realization."[104]

I have encountered a number of Christian men that so disliked the police they did not recognize the abandonment of their Christian principles, and one could see and hear the emotions in their voices, eyes, and mannerisms as they discussed their feelings about police. For some, these negative emotions toward police did not allow them to consider alternative options for addressing the problem. Howard provided potential self-realization challenges when he states, "If a man's attitude is life-negating in his relationships with those to whom he recognizes no moral responsibility, his conduct is without condemnation in his own mind."[105] There are young Black men in the community who feel it is acceptable to respond violently and physically toward police when they have a negative encounter with the police in which the police were wrong. I cannot recall when a Black man has "won" in the long run when responding physically toward police. Without question, police officers and the criminal justice system must be held accountable and change, but using hate has not been successful. It is not a new concept for the Church to take a leadership role in preparing activists to engage those in authority for the purpose of bringing about change. John Lewis chronicles the work of many such activists in his autobiographic work, *March: Book One.*

March: Book One: John Lewis

It is not a new concept to solicit the church to engage social justice issues to address oppression and many other acts of institutional racism and injustice. The March on Washington arguably was a milestone for the Civil Rights Era, bringing together thousands with diverse backgrounds to the nation's capital. John Lewis was a key figure during this time and he took a creative approach in sharing his biography, which bridged Christianity and social justice. *March: Book One* chronicled his life experiences and work as a minister of the Gospel in addressing oppression and racism from a nonviolent perspective. To attract and enlighten young readers, the book was written using comic

---

104 Ibid.
105 Ibid, 70.

book illustrations and format. Reverend Lewis went on to become a US congressman and an American icon.[106]

Early on the book illustrates the importance of prayer as marchers and protestors encounter aggressive police as they crossed a bridge. Police are carrying weapons, wearing gas masks and helmets, and they order the marchers to turn around and go back to their churches. Lewis tells Hosea Williams that they should kneel and pray as the troopers give the order to advance.[107] In this new millennium, Christians must have faith and belief in the Holy Spirit to lead and protect them in their efforts to strengthen and change the relationship between Black men and police.

As a youth, living during the time that *Separate but Equal* was ruled unconstitutional, Lewis would listen to Reverend Dr. Martin Luther King on the radio and was moved by how Dr. King applied the principles of the church to current events and called it the social gospel. What an excellent term you do not hear of today, encouraging the church to address social justice issues: social gospel. The book highlights the bus boycotts and arrests of Rosa Parks as an example of social gospel.[108] Following the activities of the Montgomery Boycott, led by Reverend King, a young Lewis stated, "Dr. King's example showed me that it was possible to do more as a minister than what I had witnessed in my own church. I was inspired."[109]

Lewis applied and was accepted to the American Baptist Theological Seminary in Nashville. I can relate to his revelation that he felt guilty reading about justice while there were people out there working to make it happen. One of the primary purposes of this study is to engage Christian men to do something about the relationship between Black men and police while still

---

106 John Lewis, Andrew Aydin, and Nate Powell. *March: Book One*. Marietta, Ga: Top Shelf Productions, 2013.
107 Ibid, 56.
108 Ibid, 58.
109 Ibid, 65.

witnessing the Good News of Jesus the Christ, believing that through the power of the Holy Spirit, both and more can be achieved.

Lewis also participated in addressing the racist law and policies that prevented Blacks from sitting at lunch counters.[110] Their protests started one week after the Greensboro, NC sit-ins. At one training and gathering to organize, more than two hundred students assembled for the peaceful protest. Part of the training for the large crowd was to make sure they knew what the rules were and how to respond to aggressive actions from the police. The protestors were given these rules, which ended with MAY GOD BLESS EACH OF YOU underlined in capital letters:[111]

DO NOT:
Strike back or curse if abused.
Laugh out.
Hold conversations with floor walker.
Leave your seat until your leader has given you permission to do so.
Block entrances to stores outside or the aisles inside.

DO:
Show yourself friendly and courteous at all times.
Sit straight; always face the counter.
Report all serious incidents to your leader.
Refer information seekers to your leader in a polite manner.
Remember the teaching of Jesus Christ, Mahatma Gandhi, and Martin Luther King. Love and nonviolence is the way.

On February 27, 1960, Lewis was arrested for the first time during a Woolworth's sit-in where the protestors were beaten by a mob while the police were conveniently late to arrive.[112] That Sunday morning, Fisk University

---

110   Ibid, 95.
111   Ibid, 97.
112   Ibid, 103.

President Dr. Stephen J. Wright addressed more than one thousand students in the University Chapel and was the first Black college president to recognize the students' courageous act and publicly stated that he stood with them.[113] The students were found guilty, refused to pay bail, and were sent to the workhouse (jail). This outraged many people throughout the country and telegrams of support came from Ralph Bunche, Eleanor Roosevelt, and Harry Belafonte. On March 3, Mayor West ordered their release.[114]

In court for their activities, the lawyers were able to say that the young people were not disturbing the police, were peaceful, and fully compliant with the law.[115] I think that this is a very important point that the defense lawyers were able to make. As we know now, Blacks eventually were able to sit at counters and became managers of the counters and stores.

For decades, Blacks have responded with riots to aggressive and illegal police actions, and today they are still responding in the same manner. Imagine if in the many protests against police killings and/or violence, protestors were instructed on what to do and what not to do with the teaching of Jesus Christ as the foundation. This study focuses on the teachings of Christ to teach young Black males about what to do when they encounter police and how to engage the local government to change policies and hire or elect leading criminal justice and law enforcement officials. The March on Washington preparation demonstrates how those who seek to address social justice by opposing oppressive policies must be prepared to engage authority.

March on Washington for Jobs and Freedom
One of the most notable and collective events that the church participated in to address social injustice was the *March on Washington for Jobs and Freedom*. It is interesting that the historic march is often abbreviated to the *March on Washington*. The last organizing efforts are documented in a brochure entitled, *Final Plans for the March on Washington for Jobs and Freedom: Organizing*

---

113 Ibid, 106.
114 Ibid, 106.
115 Ibid, 107.

Manual No. 2.[116] The pamphlet lists the ten chairman of the march: Mathew Ahmann, executive director of the National Catholic Conference for Interracial Justice; Reverend Eugene Carson Blake, vice-chairman of the Commission on Race Relations of the National Council of Churches of Christ in America; James Farmer, national director of the Congress of Racial Equality; Reverend Martin Luther King, Jr., president of the Southern Christian Leadership Conference; John Lewis, chairman of the Student Nonviolent Coordinating Committee; Rabbi Joachim Prinz, chairman of the American Jewish Congress; A. Philip Randolph, president of the Negro American Labor Council; Walter Reuther, president of the United Automobile, Aerospace and Agricultural Implement Workers of America, AFL-CIO, and chairman, Industrial Union Department, AFL-CIO; Roy Wilkins, executive secretary of the National Association for the Advancement of Colored People; and Whitney Young, executive director of the National Urban League.[117]

The brochure states that the purpose of the march was to redress old grievances and to help resolve an American crisis, noting that the livelihoods of the diverse people who were oppressed (Negros, Puerto Ricans, Mexicans, and other minorities) had been destroyed, unemployed Negros had been thrown into the streets, and the oppressed were driven to despair. More than 100,000 people were expected to convene at the Lincoln Memorial to address the government.[118]

Christian men must come to realize that aggressive nonviolent collective action is the way to address the oppressive actions of law enforcement and the criminal justice system. The level of distrust toward police and the criminal justice system has proven to be a challenge for nonviolent response to aggressive police actions. This negative perception of all law enforcement officers by many people in the Black community must be addressed by both the Black community and the police in order for nonviolent collaboration to

---

116 "Final Plans for the March on Washington for Jobs and Freedom," Organizing Manual No. 2. 1963.
117 Ibid., 3.
118 Ibid., 4.

move forward. The negative perception that often leads to violent response in the form of riots is well documented.

AFRICAN AMERICANS' HISTORICAL PERCEPTION OF LAW ENFORCEMENT

This section focuses on the historical context of the Black community's negative perceptions and lack of trust of police. I realize that many who are not in the academic arena may have very little interest in this section. I decided to keep this section in, not wanting to underestimate the interest of some to go a little "deeper" in exploring/understanding historical perspectives and insight.

This section highlights the research in the areas of church engagement in social justice, as well as research and projects focused on the relationship between the Black community and police. Historically, there have been times that the Black community has responded with violence in response to aggressive police actions, which resulted in riots. Riots have been used as a critical response to bring change to social injustice.

Robinson conducted a literature review to explain the sociological perspective of race riots in the United States.[119] Robinson's study was published in 1940. One challenge with the study is that it was not tested, but rather a review of articles and information. Robinson defines race and states that race riots are a form of race conflict.

The race riots in the early 1900s in Chicago, Washington, Tulsa, Elaine, and Longview are reviewed. Rape or other specific crimes allegedly committed by Negroes were often reported as being the reason for race riots. Another reason for race riots was Negroes and Whites competing for work. Whites attacked Negroes when the Negro got out of "his place." I selected to use the word "Negro" since it was used in the article. The significance of this study is the role of police and the impact on attitudes of Blacks towards police that may be passed down through generations. Great grandparents of today experienced police taking the sides of Whites during the riots. These grandparents communicated to their children and grandchildren about the racists actions of

---

119 Bernard F. Robinson (1941). The Sociology of Race Riots. *Phylon (1940-1956), 2*(2), 162–171.

police. The grandchildren pass on the beliefs to their children aiding some to still think of the police of today in the same manner. The number of Negroes killed in the riots always outnumbered the number of Whites. When the local police could not handle the situation, militias were often called in.

Lafree and Drass studied the annual changes in Black civil rights-related collective action and Black and White arrest rates.[120] The authors presented four competing hypotheses on the relationships between rates of collective political action and crime during the postwar. The first was that resource-mobilization theory suggests the two are unrelated. The second was that social-disorganization theories suggest that rates of crime and collective political action are positively related. The third was that various researchers predict that collective political action and crime trends are positively related, and the fourth is that using longitudinal data, researchers can test whether any relationship between collective action and crime is symmetrical. The authors used a longitudinal study to explore the connections between collective action and crime from the 1950s to the 1970s. Content analysis was used to analyze articles from the *New York Times* and the Uniform Crime Reprots (UCR) was used to analyze crime data. The UCR is crime data collected by law enforcement agencies and reported to the Federal Bureau of Investigations.

The findings show that collective action rates increased rapidly from the 1950s through the1960s, declined in the 1970s, maintained without change in the 1980's and remained relatively low during the 1990s. Arrest rates are consistently higher for Blacks than Whites and the trends for the two groups are highly correlated. The results underscore that the meanings assigned to collective action and crime are related and historically situated. While the overall trends may be true, one must be reminded that riots did take place during the 1980's and 1990's.

The historical concept of the church addressing social injustice using initiatives that may lead to aggressive police encounters, and training for those actions, is not new. Just as protestors were trained to prepare for the

---

120 Gary LaFree, and Kriss Drass. "African American Collective Action & Crime, 1955–1991." *Social Forces*, 1997, 835–853.

sit-ins, the Freedom Riders were trained to know what to do when they encountered police:

> From its founding by pacifists in 1942, the Congress of Racial Equality (CORE) was committed to practicing methods of nonviolent direct action. Similarly Rev. Jim Lawson, part of the second wave of Freedom Riders, had studied nonviolent philosophy and techniques in India and trained future leaders of the Nashville Student Movement prior to their involvement in the lunch counter sit-in campaigns. Training and role-playing in nonviolent techniques were part of the preparation for CORE's original May 4 Freedom Ride. But the greatest education came from the Rides themselves.[121]

Christian men must be assisted in developing their spiritual awareness of what is needed to strengthen relationships between Black men and police. They also need to be trained and provided with detailed information about what to do when they encounter law enforcement. These Christian men will then be better prepared to mentor young Black men not only on what to do when they encounter police, but also to begin a transformation in how they view police. Jesus trained His disciples and gave them authority to continue His work.

> Behold, I send you forth as sheep in the midst of wolves: be ye therefore wise as serpents, and harmless as doves. But beware of men: for they will deliver you up to the councils, and they will scourge you in their synagogues; And ye shall be brought before governors and kings for my sake, for a testimony against them and the Gentiles. But when they deliver you up, take no thought how or what ye shall speak: for it shall be given you in that same hour what ye shall speak. For it is not ye that speak, but the Spirit of your Father which speaketh in you.[122]

---

121 American Experience. "Freedom Riders: Threatened, Attacked, Jailed." http://www.pbs.org/wgbh/americanexperience/freedomriders/issues/victory-for-nonviolence (accessed November 25, 2014).
122 Matthew 10:16–20.

Christian men must transform from a carnal way of thinking about police and how to address the historical problem to a spiritual way of thinking. They are doing God's work under the power of the Holy Spirit that is within them and not of their own will. From this perspective, nothing but a righteous outcome will prevail.

CHURCHES AND BLACK COMMUNITY/ LAW ENFORCEMENT ENGAGEMENT

In *The Role of African-American Churches in Reducing Crime Among Black Youth,* Byron Johnson examined the hypothesis that the religious involvement of African-American youth significantly shields them from the effects of neighborhood disorder and the decay of youth crime.[123] Johnson tested his hypothesis by examining the fifth wave of data from the National Youth Survey (NYS), focusing on black respondents, given the historical as well as contemporary significance of the African-American church in the lives of Black Americans.

According to Johnson, scholars have documented that the African-American church has been an important agency of social control and organization among Black Americans and yet its potential influence for promoting prosocial behavior among Black Americans has been largely ignored by criminologists. Johnson's research explored whether church involvement diminishes the harmful effects of neighborhood decay and whether by such diminishment, black youth involvement in the church helps control criminal behavior. The article reports his findings as follows:

> First, the hypothesis about the constraining effects of church attendance on crime among Black youth received empirical support, and the effects remain significant even after controlling for non-religious social bonding/learning variables as well as socio-demographic characteristics. Second, as expected, the effects of neighborhood disorder on increasing crime among Black youth were found to be statistically

---

[123] Byron Johnson. *The Role of African-American Churches in Reducing Crime Among Black Youth.* Philadelphia: Manhattan Institute, 2001.

significant. Third, the direct effects of neighborhood disorder initially observed were reduced when black youth's religious involvement was included in the model. This finding is consistent with the hypothesis that an individual's religious involvement will weaken the detrimental effects of neighborhood disorder on youth behavior by partly mediating the neighborhood effects.[124]

US DEPARTMENT OF JUSTICE OFFICE COMMUNITY ORIENTED POLICING SERVICES

Community oriented policing (COP) is a policing philosophy and management style that gained strength nationally during President Clinton's administration. It was introduced by Michigan State University researchers and has an emphasis on creating partnerships between the community and police to address problems related to crime. Principles of COP are community engagement, problem solving, and partnerships.[125] The US Department of Justice created the Community Oriented Policing Consortium and sponsored workshops on police community collaboration throughout the nation. The National Organization of Black Law Enforcement Executives (NOBLE) was a key partner in the COP Consortium. The US Department of Justice also created the Office of Community Oriented Policing Services.

The US Department of Justice Office of Community Oriented Policing Services (COPS) has funded initiatives aimed at using faith organizations for strengthening the relationships with police for more than two decades. While I have not worked with any of these initiatives, I worked with the Department of Justice and COPS office (Community Policing Consortium) on numerous community engagement and problem solving initiatives for nearly a decade (from 1993 to 2002).

The following information was retrieved from a document published by the US Department of Justice Office of Community Oriented Policing Services. It is entitled *Making the Match: Law Enforcement, the Community and the*

---

124 Ibid, 5.
125 David L.Carter and Louis A. Radalet. *Police and The Community.* Michigan: Prentice Hall Publishing, 2001.

Value Based Initiative. The Value-Based Initiative (VBI) was a COPS-funded strategy that emphasized training and technical assistance for problem-solving on a grass roots level. Below is a selection VBI collaboration that focused on strengthening the relationship between police and the faith communities. More information can be found on the US Department of Justice website.[126]

Building a Generation, the Redlands, California
This VBI project was the Police Chief's Clergy Advisory Council. The council consisted of about 10 respected area faith leaders and functioned as a kind of spiritual SWAT team. The members met monthly with the chief and were also available on an on-call basis as needed.

Ministers Against Crime (MAC)
This program was part of the VBI project in Fort Worth, Texas. MAC helped the police keep potentially volatile situations from escalating to violence and conducted nightly crime patrols.

Cops and Clergy Network (CCN)
CCN a coalition of police, clergy and other Faith-Based Organizations (FBO) leaders and was established in 1998 by a minister who believed that law enforcement officials and people of faith had more in common than they might think.

Faith Leaders Ministerial Academies
Faith Leaders Ministerial Academies was a generic name for a police sponsored training program for clergy and other FBO leaders with the purpose of educating clergy about local law enforcement.

Another study funded by the US Department of Justice Office of COPS was "Victimization, Contact with Police, and Attitudes toward the Police."[127] The study confirms citizens' attitudes toward police are important when

---

126 Mary Gordon. *Making the Match: Law Enforcement, the Faith Community and the Value-Based Initiative.* Washington: US Department of Justice, Office of Community Oriented Policing Services, 2003.
127 Kenneth and Raymond Sparks. "Victimization, Contact with Police, and Neighborhood Conditions: Reconsidering African American and Hispanic Attitudes toward the Police." *Police Practice and Research* 9, No. 5 (December 2008): 395–415.

assessing police in a community. This study found that race was related to police satisfaction and Blacks and Hispanics reported less satisfaction with police. It is important to note that the study found that the perception of the quality of life was a stronger predictor of police satisfaction.

BLACK MALES AND POLICE RELATIONS

This section includes highights of select research conducted primarily by university professors. While some of the articles are rather old by academic standards, the articles exemplify that the study of Black male and police relations is not new. I find it interesting that while many in universities have long studied the problem, things have not only changed, but in some respect became more problematic. The term qualitative refers to research that is more subjective and is based on analysis of interviews and case studies. The term quantitative usually refers to analysis of statistics. It is interesting to reflect on some of the research in earlier years, considering the increased publicity of police shootings.

Engel (2005) suggests that perceptions of injustice are not based solely on outcomes of police encounters, but on perceptions of police. In other words, even if Black males have favorable police encounters, their ingrained perceptions of police may outweigh actual experiences, continuing their lack of confidence in police.[128]

A second qualitative article, "Measuring Influences on Public Opinion of the Police Using Time-Series Data: Results of a Pilot Study", brings additional insight to people's perceptions of police by addressing the following questions: Do contacts between police and citizens have a ripple effect as people tell their families, neighbors, and friends about police? And, are perceptions influenced by exposure to information through mass media?[129] The research relied on three sources of time-series data collected across nine four-week periods in five police precincts across New York City.

---

128 Robin Engel. "Citizens' Perceptions of Distributive and Procedural Injustice During Traffic Stops with Police." *Journal of Research in Crime and Delinquency*, 2005: 445–481.
129 Joel Miller, Robert Davis, Nicole Henderson, John Markovic, and Christopher Oritz. "Measuring Influences on Public Opinion of the Police Suing Time Series Data: Results of a Pilot Study." *Police Quarterly*, 2005: 394–401.

The data was captured through consumer surveys, community surveys, and media tracking, along with timing the data collection. Both consumer satisfaction and public opinion were positive and showed minimal variation through time. Over the nine months, there were no substantial changes either in public opinion or in the nature of police public encounters. Public opinion was fairly stable across nine consecutive months despite some notable variations in media coverage. This suggests that variation in news coverage of the police may not easily sway views of them in the absence of any major scandals. Obviously the recent media coverage of Black male shootings by police may play a significant role in the results if this study were to take place over the past nine months. Although the focus of this study has direct relationship to my research questions, the study is not detailed enough to provide sound information. Demographics of the precincts and participants would have assisted as well.

"Debunking the Myth of Officer Friendly" is a quantitative study analyzing perceptions of minority youth toward police.[130] The study took place between the fall of 1993 and 1994. Participants were recruited from three high schools, a boys and girls club, a summer basketball league, and a housing authority summer work program. The study was open to males age sixteen and seventeen, or within three months of the target age. A total of 125 Black males participated in the study, which took place within five towns of a suburban county in central New Jersey.

A majority of the Black males reported experiencing the police as a repressive rather than facilitative agent. The Black males strongly believed that race plays a role in police-citizen contacts. There was also concern about the risk of Black males developing negative self-images. Findings suggest that repressive police encounters may reinforce negative attitudes toward police, learned through socialization. This study did not report high levels of delinquency, nor did it report antisocial or delinquent values.

These studies support a compelling case for using the Church to strengthen the relationships between Black men and police. The findings of these articles

---

130 Delores Jones-Brown. "Debunking the Myth of Officer Friendly." *Journal of Contemporary Criminal Justice*, 2000: 209–229.

demonstrate a need to further explore what impact negative attitudes have on the outcome of police encounters and whether an initiative will reduce negative outcomes between young Black males and police. As shown in some of these articles, Blacks' negative perceptions of police are well documented.

Taslitz begins to move beyond Blacks' perceptions of encounters with police.[131] *Respect and the fourth amendment* ventures into an area not covered by other literature reviewed.[132] The author addresses respect for the fourth amendment as a method of analyzing police searches and seizures. The question that prompted the research was, "Why do many minority communities experience rage at certain police search and seizure practices involving their communities' members?"[133] Most members of the community at large oppose illegally obtained evidence, yet many members do not consider illegal searches a major offense if crime is being controlled.[134]

I think that this research brings up an interesting topic for debate for the Black communit today. To what extent is the Black community concerned with crime, especially Black on Black crime? In addition, how much of their individual rights are some in the Black community willing to give up, reducing victimization? There is still the reality that many in the Black community are still being victimized by all levels of criminal offenders. Taslitz concludes by stating there is a gap in research addressing respect and treating others fairly beyond search and seizure.[135]

Lundman addresses the issue of vehicle searches by police.[136] According to his study, citizens report concern over legal and extralegal factors of race, ethnicity, and gender when it comes to traffic stop encounters that lead to

---

131 Andrew E. Taslitz. "Respect and the Fourth Amendment." *The Journal of Law & Criminology*, 2003: 15–101.
132 Ibid.
133 Ibid, 15.
134 Ibid.
135 Ibid.
136 Richard Lundman. "Driver Race, Ethnicity, and Gender and Citizen Reports of Vehicle Searches by Police and Search Hits: Toward a Triangulated Scholarly Understanding." *The Journal of Criminal Law and Delinquency*, 2004: 309–345.

search and seizure by police. This review of literature revealed research that focuses on Blacks' perceptions of police, where those perceptions come from, high incarceration rates of Black males, and concern that search and seizure practices at traffic stops are biased. There is a gap in scholarly research that seeks to understand if Black males' perceptions of police, once stopped by police, lead to negative interpersonal communications that fuel police arrests that would not otherwise have taken place.

THEORETICAL FOUNDATION

Theory provides the philosophical stance informing the methodology and therefore providing context for the process while grounding logic and criteria (characteristics).[137] A much more basic statement that I often use with my lower level college students is, theory provides a framework to assist in understanding why something happens and can also address why some people commit crimes and other acts. As an example, do criminals commit crime due to their environment, or heredity? Do some people commit crime because they see it, experience it and learn it? Do some peope commit crime because of the genes that they are born with? Epistemology is the theory of knowledge that is embedded in the theory and therefore the methodology.[138] Theory can also explain behaviors beyond crime. This section describes the theoretical framework of culture conflict theory to gain insight to why many in the Black community distrust police.

Culture conflict theory brings insight into why and how Black males develop these negative perceptions of police. Culture conflict theory has many premises. One is that, over a period of time, behavior becomes accepted within a culture as a norm and violation of those conduct norms arouses group reaction.[139] The criminologist Thorsten Sellin originally formulated the

---

137 Michael J.Crotty. *The Foundations of Social Research: Meaning and Perspective in the Research Process.* Thousand Oaks: SAGE, 1998.
138 Ibid.
139 Shaun Gabbidon and Helen Taylor Greene. *Race and Crime.* Thousand Oaks, CA: Sage Publications, Inc., 2005.

theory in the late 1930s.[140] All societies have conduct norms and these norms may differ from one culture to another. What may be a violation of a conduct norm in one society (community) may not be a violation in another. A leading proposition of culture conflict theory is that conflict between authorities and subjects occurs when behavioral differences between authorities and subjects are compounded by cultural differences.[141] Using this theory to synthesize the problem, one can begin with Blacks' and Whites' perceptions of police.

There is a conduct norm in much of the White community to respect, trust, and obey the police. In accordance with culture conflict theory, this conduct norm may be a violation in the Black community due to the history between Blacks and police. This negative perception of police is what Sellin refers to as primary culture conflict.[142]

In White communities, historically, police are seen as protectors of the community and are looked up to for protection, justice, and equality. In Black communities, historically, police are seen as protectors of the White community and enforcers of laws that were often oppressive to the Black community. As recently as the 1960s, there is accepted documentation that police enforced laws that were oppressive toward Blacks. As oppressive laws diminished, the negative perceptions of police continued within the Black community.[143]

This evolutionary process of social differentiation is what Sellin refers to as secondary conflicts.[144] The premise is that over a period of time, behavior becomes accepted within a culture as a norm and violations of those conduct norms lead to an arousal of group reaction that is displayed when someone in the Black community voices support of the police. This arousal originates

---

140 Ibid.
141 Ailen A. Liska. *Perspectives on Deviance*. Englewood Cliffs: Prentice-Hall, 1987.
142 Ibid.
143 Tendayi Viki, Michelle J. Culmer, Anja Eller, and Dominic Abrams. "Race and Willingness to Cooperate with the Police: The Roles of Quality of Contact, Attitudes Towards the Behavior and Subjective Norms." *British Journal of Social Psychology*, 2006: 285–302.
144 Shaun L. Gabbidon and Helen Taylor Greene. *Race and Crime*. Thousand Oaks, CA: Sage Publications, Inc., 2005.

in Blacks who do not trust the police and is directed toward Blacks who support them. The individual who supports the police may be seen as less than supportive of his/her own community. A recent example of this is when in response to *Black Lives Matter*, if a Black person publicly states *All Lives Matter*, they are seen as not supportive of pro Black issues. Another example is when someone Black brings up the issue of Black on Black crime during the discussion of the shooting of Black males by police.

4

RESEARCH METHODOLOGIES

THE RESEARCH DESIGN has a lot to do with the success of a dissertation project. I used a triangulation research design composed of pre/post surveys, small group discussion, and a case study. I observed and documented attitudinal changes that came from members and visitors of the Men's Ministry in/and or connected with the Cup of Salvation Church, as well as selected subjects who are interested in improving the relationship between Black males and police.

An ethnographic approach was used to study participants' interest and ability to mentor young Black men on how to improve relationships with police based on Christian principles. According to Bordens and Abbott, "a researcher becomes immersed in the behavioral or social system being studied."[145] In this sense, I become partially immersed in the lives of the men at the Cup of Salvation via participant observation, participating at select church activities while using a systematic procedure to introduce information and evaluate attitudinal change, as discussed by Bordens and Abbott.

A triangulation research design of mixed methodologies (quantitative and qualitative) was utilized to measure and evaluate the results. This took place via field survey using a pre-post Likert scale questionnaire, a focus group

---

145 Kenneth Bordens and Bruce Abbott. *Research Design and Methods: A Process Approach.* Boston: McGraw-Hill, 2005, pg. 209.

discussion, and a single case study. Triangulation involves the use of more than one approach to the investigation of a hypothesis and enhances confidence in the findings.

In field surveys, researchers directly question participants about behaviors, attitudes, and beliefs; inferences are drawn about the factors underlying their behavior. Likert rating survey scales are widely used in attitudinal measurement research and provide a series of statements to which participants can indicate degrees of agreement or disagreement.

A focus group is a common qualitative research technique used by researchers and typically consists of a small number of participants. In a focus group the researchers ask participants for responses to open-ended questions that convey their thoughts and/or feelings. A focus group can offer insights consistent with those shared by the broader population. Focus groups are more useful when the researcher is looking for open feedback.[146]

Case history is a descriptive technique in which the researcher observes and reports on a single case (or few cases), which allows for in-depth study. Case study allows for speculation of causes. It is ideal to use in a triangulation research design.

---

146 Ibid., 243.

FIELD EXPERIENCE-IMPLEMENTING THE PROGRAM

The Reverend Dr. Martin Luther King, Jr. introduced a Christian perspective of nonviolence to change systemic racism and discrimination in the United States. Reverend King used Christian principles to educate individuals on how to mentor others about what to do when faced with aggression while protesting. His strategies were much larger than protesting as he garnered national and international support through media attention. The process he introduced also had an economic impact on many southern communities. This mighty man of God fostered an attitudinal change from fear and violence to confidence and aggressive nonviolence among those who challenged the status quo.

The field experience in this proejct delineates the steps taken to develop and implement an intervention program that would educate and spiritually prepare Christian men to mentor young Black men on how they can strengthen their relationship with police. **The goal of the field experience/program is to enlighten Christian men on the difference between viewing police and police relations from a carnal-minded perspective to a spiritual and scriptural-minded perspective.** The assumption is that if Christian men have an attitudinal change about their approach and understanding of law enforcement authority, then they can educate young Black men on how to change their perceptions of police and what to do when they encounter police. In addition, another goal is to educate Christian men on how to systematically influence police policy and police perceptions of Black men in their community. While this project does not focus on post-incarceration assistance and prison recidivism reduction, limited strategies are provided.

It is extremely important for church leadership to prepare the entire body for any social justice initiative. While all members may not be personally engaged, the entire body should be equipped and prepared. The body must understand the relevance to church doctrine, biblical principles, and spiritual foundation.

The original plan called for three steps of intervention and program design, Bible study, a sermon, and a workshop. During the monthly Men's Ministry Saturday meeting prior to the scheduled workshop, an announcement to remind and recruit men for the workshop was permitted. That announcement turned into a two-hour discussion about Black men and the criminal justice system. The purpose of this multistep approach was to begin to educate the entire congregation on the need to strengthen relationships between Black men and police, demonstrate the need in the community, begin a spiritual-minded transition to address the issue of Black male/police relations, and foster support for the workshop.

BIBLE STUDY

The Cup of Salvation convenes for Sunday school and church service every Sunday. Corporate prayer is held on Wednesday nights from 7:00 to 8:00. Corporate prayer is coordinated by the intercessory prayer team and usually involves those attending, standing in a circle and reading prepared prayers with selected themes. Time is usually given for testimonies and prayer requests. Youths meet on Wednesday evenings to participate in choir rehearsal, Bible study, or group activities. Friday nights are reserved for Bible study (from 7:00 to 8:30). Someone from Ecclesiastical leadership is selected to lead Bible Study. The first Saturday of every month is reserved for the Men's Ministry and the Second Sunday of every month is reserved for Women's Ministry. Each is scheduled for two hours, 10:00 a.m. to 12:00 noon.

I was scheduled to lead Bible Study on October 25, 2013. I used the opportunity to lay a foundation of community engagement to address the issue of police and Black male relationships and other social needs of the community.

The purpose of the session was to confirm the need for the church to reach out to the community. While only select groups may address certain social justice issues within the community, the entire church body should be educated on the needs and issues.

All attendees were given a handout of the material I presented.[147] They were asked to review the material throughout the week after the information was covered. After opening with prayer, the material was covered in a discussion-style session. The vision and mission statement of the church was read first. The primary theme of the church is to "Reach them, teach them, and set them free." The leadership of the church has selected a specific geographical area to directly impact in Durham and it has been titled the Lazarus Territory. While not exact, the Lazarus territory primarily covers zip code 27703. A wide range of demographics concerning crime, population, education, and social economics in the area were covered. Some highlights included poor education rates for Black children, especially Black males. African Americans were also on the low end of social economics.

The information was well received and some were surprised to see the challenging statistics related to low education achievement. The session was closed with many providing words of thanks for the information. The Youth Pastor said he now had specific information to plan his strategies. A member of the intercessory prayer team advised me that she now had specific points to emphasize for prayer.

SERMON

In October, I was advised that I would have the opportunity to preach in November.[148] The sermon used the Old Testament foundation scripture of this study for its foundation. The title of the sermon was "Moses and the Plight of Young Black Men in the United States and Authority." The sermon began by comparing the plight of Black men in the United States to a

---

147 See Appendix B.
148 See Appendix A.

sickness that must be diagnosed, a solution identified, and an intervention prescribed and implemented. A synopsis of the life of Moses was given by reading select scriptures in a narrative format. Moses was described as a murderer who ran from authority, was nurtured and later used as a servant of God for mighty work. There is a parallelism in the story to Black men who have done wrong, but can still be used by God for mighty work in the community. Many Christian men have been incarcerated or arrested. They can be used to mentor other Christian men about police encounters and the criminal justice system. Statistics of Black males in the United States and Durham community were highlighted.

WORKSHOP RECRUITMENT

The title of the workshop was selected from the research project title. It was derived from a combination of the subject matter and the focus of the Doctor of Ministry (D.Min) cohort title *Christian Leadership in the Epilogue to the Post Modern Era*. The title of the D.Min research project and workshop is *African American Men and Police: A Christ Solution for the New Millennium*. The content of the workshop was based on my previous research experience, experience as a mentor to young Black men for more than twenty-five years, thirty years of experience in the criminal justice field, and more than eight years as a minister of the Gospel of Jesus the Christ.

Recruitment for the workshop focused on members of the Cup Family, Cup of Salvation Deliverance Church and a North Carolina Central University Criminal Justice class. The Cup Family is comprised of five churches that have an average membership ranging from fifteen people to two hundred people. Announcements were sent to Cup Family churches. For the Cup of Salvation Deliverance Church, announcements were made in church on Sundays during the month of January and sent via e-mail to men who were members of the church. I also made an announcement at a Law Enforcement Theory and Policy course that I taught. The announcement included statistics on Black male incarceration and arrests rates. (See Appendix C.)

MEN'S MINISTRY MEETING DISCUSSION

An unexpected and unplanned intervention opportunity took place at the Men's Ministry meeting in January. I was given permission to recruit for the workshop that was scheduled to take place at the monthly meeting in February. After statistics of Black males and the criminal justice system were given and the title of the workshop shared, an emotional and passionate discussion took place that lasted the full two hours of the scheduled meeting. The intention was to give a five-minute overview and invitation. Since this two-hour discussion was not intended, documentation did not take place. The conversations ranged from microlevel personal encounters to the desire to assist men who had been incarcerated. Most of the conversation was about negative perceptions of police, but some of the conversation focused on the need to do something about Black-on-Black crime. A few men referenced the need to teach young Black males what to do when police stop them.

WORKSHOP

In November 2013, I discussed the concept of the workshop and asked the permission of the Senior Executive Pastor of Cup of Salvation Deliverance Church, Apostle Dr. Johnny Holloway, to give the workshop. He had already been informed of the Doctor of Ministry studies and focus of the research and intervention. Apostle Holloway expressed support of the studies and project. He informally agreed to the intervention in the form of a workshop. An informal discussion was then held with the Executive Pastor, Versal Mason. The Men's Ministry was one of the ministries under his direction. He informally agreed to support the Men's Ministry's hosting of the workshop and asked me to seek Minister Jake Robertson's approval. Minister Jake Robertson was directly responsible for the coordination of the Men's Ministry. Minister Jake Robertson was familiar with the D.Min. studies and agreed to host the workshop. An e-mail was then sent to all three pastors and all three agreed to have the Men's Ministry host the workshop. It was agreed that the workshop would be held on the first Saturday in February.

The Men's Ministry traditionally meets on the first Saturday of every month from 10:00 a.m. to 12:00 noon. A discussion usually takes place in a classroom in the Cup Center and is open to all men and young men of any age, and visitors occasionally attend. While the attendance varies, it typically ranges between five and fifteen people. The topics vary, usually addressing issues related to Christian men, and they are usually based on scripture.

WORKSHOP MATERIAL

Throughout the month of January I conducted research and put together information for the workshop. Information was placed in a two-pocket folder supplied by North Carolina Central University Department of Criminal Justice-Institute for Homeland Security and Workforce Development.[149] The department's logo appeared on the folders. The material in the folder was color coded to simplify referral throughout the workshop. In the left side of the folder from top to bottom were:

- o agenda with times in gray
- o facilitator biography in green
- o PowerPoint presentation (two slides per page) in yellow

My business card was placed in the business card slot located on the right side of the folder. In the right side of the folder from top to bottom were:

- 5x4 note pad from the Rural Domestic Preparedness Consortium
- information brochure from National Association of Blacks in Criminal Justice
- trifold pamphlet *What Every Christian Should Know about Authority*
- Consent to Participate in Research form in salmon
- pre-survey in yellow
- *Black Criminal Stereotypes and Racial Profiling* article in green
- Workshop evaluation form in light blue

---

149 See Appendix D.

The PowerPoint presentation was eighteen pages long with slides on front and back. I served as the project director for the Rural Domestic Preparedness Consortium (RDPC) for NCCU. RDPC provides public safety training for rural communities throughout the country (ruraltraining.org). Information on RDPC was included. The National Association of Blacks in Criminal Justice headquarters is located at North Carolina Central University and was included to exemplify professionals committed to social justice and professionalism in the criminal justice field. *What Every Christian Should Know about Authority* provides biblical-based foundations and discussions on authority for Christians to follow. Dr. Dale Robbins wrote the article (1994, www.victorious.org). The workshop evaluation was designed to capture written information that could be shared during the small group discussion at the end of the workshop. The small group discussion was to serve as part of the triangulation research design. Participants were also given a copy of the book *Destiny Denied: A Black Man's Prevention and Survival Guide To Police Encounters*, which I authored.

ROOM DESIGN

The workshop was held in the Cup Center at the Cup of Salvation Deliverance Church. The Cup Center is a multipurpose room with a kitchen attached to it. Cup Center staff set up the room the night prior to the workshop. The room was set up in a horseshoe or U shape. There were approximately three rectangular tables on each side with two on the back end. Approximately twenty-five chairs were set around the tables. The PowerPoint projector was located at the head of the table with the projector pointed toward the wall. When facing the front of the room, a table was located to the left with coffee, drinks, fruit, and snacks. The workshop was scheduled to begin at 9:30 a.m. I arrived to set up at 8:30 a.m. Set up included placing folders on tables, making coffee, setting up the food table, setting up a sign-in sheet on a table and setting up the laptop and PowerPoint projector.

Outstretched Hands Community Development Corporation (OHCDC) sponsored the workshop. The food and drinks were donated by OHCDC. The

501c3 nonprofit organization focuses on social justice issues related to poverty, literacy, juvenile justice, and senior citizen needs in the Research Triangle area of North Carolina. OHCDC also supports community and ministry work in Kenya, Uganda, and surrounding countries in Africa. OHCDC was birthed out of CSDC. I serve as the Executive Vice President of the organization.

WORKSHOP DELIVERY

A minimum sample of twenty people was desired with a preference for twenty-five. Only five men were present at 9:30. By approximately 9:45, a total of ten men had arrived. By 9:50, fifteen men had arrived. A total of twenty men had arrived by 10:00. All of the men appeared to be African American. I was familiar with all of them, but one. One male had a light complexion and could have been of mixed nationality, possibly Hispanic. From personal knowledge, the ages ranged from approximately sixteen to seventy. Two young men age eighteen came in approximately one hour late and stayed for approximately two hours. They came as a sign of support for me. I mentored one of the young men in a formal program for "at risk" youth. He describes himself as someone who has sold drugs, who struggled to not join a gang, and who has a dislike for police. A friend accompanied him. I acknowledged his presence and used him in an exercise, telling him in front of everyone that he knew I loved him. Throughout the workshop, men were called up for small visuals, or exercises. A more complete sample analysis is provided in the data analysis section.

I delayed starting the workshop until 9:50 due to attendance. From 9:30 to 9:50 the welcome, prayer, praise and worship, introductions and pre-survey were scheduled. Someone was asked to volunteer to open with prayer. Executive Pastor Versal Mason was asked to give a welcome on behalf of the Cup of Salvation Men's Ministry and then lead the men in a song. Most, if not all, of the men participated in the song. I then gave a two to three minute welcome speech and directed participants to look at everything in the folder, giving them a brief description of its contents. The men were told where the bathrooms and exits were located. Participants were asked to write their names on a small slip of paper for a $25.00 gift card drawing to be held at the end of the workshop. Participants were directed to the Human Subjects Form. I reviewed it with them and then asked them to sign it. The Human Subjects Form was then collected. The purpose of the Human Subjects form was to inform the men that the workshop was also part of a research study and to formally get the consent to use information from the workshop. This of course would not be necessary in workshops facitliated by your church, or in your community. The men were asked to introduce themselves. A brief overview of OHCDC and a review of the agenda were presented.

The next section was scheduled to last from 9:50 to 10:15. Due to the delayed start, the session was running about thirty minutes behind. The Old Testament and New Testament foundation scriptures were shared and a brief conversation took place. Exodus 2:11–15 and Luke 22:47–52 were the scriptures read and discussed using the King James translation. Participants were then asked to briefly share any of their experiences with police if they wished to. It was anticipated that these would last approximately ten minutes. This session ended up taking about twenty minutes. A couple of participants described what they perceived as negative encounters with police. Their comments sparked conversations and debates about negative issues they had with police. A couple of the participants started speaking rather loudly and long, demonstrating their emotions about their experiences and beliefs, which were not positive. I decided it was important to let them express themselves and not end their comments and the discussion due to time.

One male who appeared to be between the ages of fifty and sixty demonstrated a higher level of dislike for the police. He expressed comments like "they are corrupt" and they "cannot be trusted." He referenced being a victim of racist police officers. His voice was elevated and he was pointing his finger with a shaking motion. A couple of the other men gave personal testimonies of what they considered racist and/or unjust police stops and encounters.

I then gave a two to three minute overview of *Destiny Denied*, highlighting sections of the book that would be used for the workshop. After discussing *Destiny Denied*, participants were given five minutes to think of and research additional scriptures that focus on authority. Many had bibles on their tablets and cell phones. A few men had hard copies, and a couple of bibles were retrieved from one of the classrooms adjacent to the Cup Center. Approximately four men shared scriptures that relate to authority with brief discussions. I had a list just in case it was needed. Due to the extended conversation about personal experiences with police, the workshop was then about forty-five minutes behind schedule.

The agenda handout and the PowerPoint presentation were a couple of slides out of order. As an example, the agenda listed the PowerPoint presentation in this order: foundational scriptures, personal experiences, benefits of improved Black male police relationships, and then *Destiny Denied*. All of this was scheduled to be covered from 9:50 to 10:15. However, the PowerPoint presentation contained slides in this order: foundational scriptures, *Destiny Denied*, the Dale Robbins Article, and the benefits of improved Black male community relations. For the most part, I covered the information in the order of the PowerPoint presentation. The overview of the Robbins article primarily focused on *The Concern with Authority, Rebellion Disrespects all Authority and Corrupt Authority* at my discretion.

Nine slides titled *Why Are We Here?* were then covered. Information covered in the slides included:

1. Statistics on the number of Black males incarcerated and their impacts (Center for American Progress article excerpt)
2. A Survey of Racial Attitudes in Cincinnati (article excerpt)
3. Police-Community Relations in a Majority-Black City (article quote)
4. Durham Homicide Rates and Black Men (Bulleted Statistics-Durham Crime Report)
5. Quote referencing the fact that police get little credit for good performance and it negatively impacts police encounters (*Journal of Research in Crime and Delinquency*)
6. Homicide rates related to Black males (Bureau of Justice Statistics)
7. Uniform Crime Report Statistics
8. Black criminal stereotypes and racial profiling article quote (Welch 2007)

A copy of the Welch (2007) article was included in the folder material and reviewed in more detail. All of the slides contained citations or website addresses at the bottom. The next slide covered was entitled *Our Approach To Address The Problem: From Carnal To Spiritual Mindedness*. Romans 8:5–10 was read.

A discussion of the scripture took place. This was a pivotal and important point of the workshop to challenge Christian men to think of police relations from a spiritual perspective. I provided a brief exegesis of the scripture. There was limited discussion due to men not having much response. They listened in a manner that I would describe as intent while focusing their eyes on me. A few men would nod their head in acknowledgment as I spoke.

A brief discussion was scheduled at this point in the workshop as shown on a slide that was projected. The slide was entitled "Ten Minute Break" and had a picture of a stopwatch ringing. The workshop was now approximately one hour behind and participants were advised to get something to drink and eat as needed and we would break for a few minutes. The time was approximately 11:40 and the break was scheduled for 10:40.

The next slide was entitled "Origins of Perceptions of Police." A brief discussion was held about the bullet points on the left-hand side of the slide. Those points included: slave police, Jim Crow law police, '60s civil rights, corrupt police experiences, abusive police experiences, media, music, and family perceptions. On the right-hand side of the slide was an excerpt that provided a brief history of slave police. There was limited verbal response to the slide.

The next four slides were entitled "Advances of Blacks in Criminal Justice." The first slide contained seven major cities in North Carolina that have had a Black police chief. On the right-hand side of the slide was a picture of Raleigh Police Chief Cassandra-Deck Brown. The next slide listed a number of other agencies and organizations in the criminal justice system in which African Americans were able to achieve significant advances. They included referencing the former head of the NC Highway Patrol, Durham District Attorney, and the US Marshal for the Eastern District of NC (his picture was on the right side of the slide). It also highlighted that the US Attorney General was an African American. The next slide highlighted criminal justice professional organizations that represented issues related to African Americans. Those organizations included the National Organization of Black Law Enforcement Executives (NOBLE), National Association of Blacks in Criminal Justice, and North State Law Enforcement Officers Associations.

One participant referenced that maybe most of the leadership had "sold out," or were "Uncle Toms." I replied that maybe some had, but I knew several who had suffered at the hands of racism in the profession and that is why the organizations were started. I then stated that I was far from an "Uncle Tom" during my tenure as police chief. Several attendees laughed in response.

The next two slides were entitled "Mentoring Young Black Males on Police Relationships." The first slide gave three cited definitions of mentor and mentoring. The second slide listed six biblical examples of mentoring relationships and Proverbs 22:6 on the left-hand side. On the right-hand side were contemporary strategies for mentoring that included informal one-on-one relationships, formal one-on-one relationships, family discussions, small group discussions, and church sessions.

At this point time had become an issue. It was 12:10 p.m. and the post survey and closing remarks were scheduled to take place from 12:20 to 12:30 and then the small group discussion from 12:30 to 12:55. Participants were referred to their copy of *Destiny Denied*. They were directed to pages 72–88, which discussed police officer diversity. The PowerPoint slide listed ten different types of officers that are discussed in the book: White/friend officer, officer "sista" B/F, officer brother b/m, officer confused b/m, officer political, officer White/Black political, officer Klan, officer whatever, officer gung-ho, and cross police types. Participants were informed that they may encounter many different officers with different motives and experiences. Participants listened intently with some nodding their heads as they turned the pages of the book.

Participants were then directed to pages 108–138 of *Destiny Denied*. The PowerPoint slide was entitled "What To Do and Not To Do During Police Encounters." A subtitle on the left side was titled "Driving While Black" and included the following recommendations:

- Wait for instructions
- Vehicle registration placement
- Reaching for your wallet

- Reaching under seat/in back
- Roll window down
- Hands 10 and 2
- Tone of speech
- Respect the badge

On the right-hand of the same slide was the subtitle "Walking While Black." The following bullet points were listed:

- Comply with officer
- Do not run
- Check your attitude
- Have government ID easily accessible
- Safety "pat down" vs. search
- Be aware of your environment
- Know who you are with

As I provided brief comments on each bullet, some participants whispered comments to the person sitting next to them. On a couple of the bullets I provided examples, calling participants up for demonstrations. As an example, a participant was called up to simulate the difference between a search and a "pat down." I asked the participant to "assume the position" and participants laughed as he immediately raised his hands, spread his legs, and leaned on the wall. I then discussed how a safety "pat down" is different. In a pat down, only things the officer feels could be considered a weapon can be taken out of the pocket. This is compared to feeling something soft, even if it feels like a small package, potentially illegal drugs. We then discussed how some officers will first ask individuals to empty their pockets to determine if weapons are present, causing illegal drugs to be shown, if present. There were several comments and questions about individual rights and personal experiences. I advised them that I wanted to limit my comments from a legal perspective. A conversation on the importance of giving up some individual rights for the safety of others and the solving of crimes lasted for three to five minutes.

A two to three minute conversation took place about the next slide entitled "Stupid Reasonable Suspicious Actions." The topics on this slide included:

- Playing loud music
- Drinking from a brown bag/small cup
- Smoking marijuana in the car/public
- Not coming to a complete stop
- Expired tags
- Illegally tinted windows
- Speeding in a residential area
- Stopping before a check point

A comment at the bottom of the slide stated "Especially knowing your license has been suspended/revoked, or there may be potential warrants, you have been drinking, etc." There were several small conversations between neighbors as each item was discussed. Most men nodded their head in agreement and a couple commented about personal experiences. I placed emphasis that these recommendations were not to help individuals circumvent the law while seeking to do something illegal, but rather to remind others that their actions can lead to reasonable suspicion and justify legitimate stops and encounters.

The next slide was entitled "Black Men, Women, and the Law." Bullet points provided were statutory rape, domestic violence, jealousy, and stalking. The men were informed that these are very important situations that young men must be mentored on. A conversation of approximately one minute was held on the sex offender status that can result from consensual sex with underage females, even if the ages are close.

The final two slides provided measures and programs on how citizens can become engaged with local police departments and programs that can assist men who have been in prison or have arrest records. One participant said that he was most interested in the organizations that can help those who have been incarcerated. One participant referenced that he did not know that police departments have "ride-a-long" programs. Another participant said that he had participated in a prison ministry program at the church he attends. At this point participants were advised that the workshop was over and I asked if they had any questions. There were no questions and someone said "Good information," and several attendees applauded.

Participants were given ten minutes to complete the post survey and the surveys were collected. Someone volunteered to give a closing prayer. Participants were advised that we were about to quickly move into the small group discussion and that it would be recorded. They were given a couple of minutes to stretch, use the bathroom, and get something to drink.

FOCUS GROUP DISCUSSION

Participants were advised that the recording was about to be turned on.[150] We were scheduled to have twenty-five minutes for the small group discussion and it was now 12:45. We were scheduled to have the drawing, closing comments, and prayer at 12:55. Everything was scheduled to end at 1:00. Participants were asked to take out the light blue form from their folder with the title "Workshop Evaluation." They were asked to write their thoughts on the evaluation and to not put their name on the form. At the top of the form was a statement, advising them to do the same. Participants were previously informed that the workshop had two purposes: to provide them with information and to assist with my research project. At the beginning of the morning, they were advised that the small group session would serve as part of the research project evaluation process.

Participants were advised that the questions on the worksheet and the PowerPoint served only as a guide to stimulate discussion. The guide questions asked were:

What are the greatest strengths of the workshop?
What would you change?
Would you recommend the workshop to others? Why, or why not?
Other comments?

---

150 Appendix E

Participants provided their feedback. The small group discussion and pre/post surveys were used in combination with a case study for the triangulation evaluation methodology. A data analysis of all three was performed and the results are reported in the workshop data analysis section of this book.

The men were thanked for their time and participation. Someone thanked me for addressing the topic and providing the workshop. Several men then applauded. The drawing was held for the $25 gift card. The winner took the gift card and later gave it back as a donation. The random selection for the case study took place.

As men were dismissed, some church members stayed behind and assisted with clean up. Approximately seven men came to me and said "Good job," providing some additional comments. One stated that a break was really needed and then commented he understood the time constraint.

Another attendee said that the information toward the end was very important (post incarceration assistance) and what he was most interested in, but we rushed through that information. He advised he was very interested in helping those who had been in prison. Another commented that it should have been an all day workshop. It took me about thirty minutes to pack up and assist with cleaning up.

MY ASSESSMENT
Overall things went well and information seemed to be well received. It is clear that more time was needed. I was originally concerned with getting men to commit for a longer time on Saturday, and I still think that would have been an issue. One way to address that is to have the men's organization fully sponsor the workshop as their organization's activity. This may help with recruitment and time commitment of six to eight hours. If your church and community are considering a similar workshop, I actually recommend a series of sessions. If sponsored by an organization, providing lunch may also assist with participants committing to a full day. Clearly, expecting to start on time was a problem. The Cup of Salvation Men's Ministry gatherings traditionally started at 10:00, and this workshop was scheduled for 9:30.

Although I anticipated some hostility toward police, I did not expect the level that took place at the workshop. This was probably because I was familiar with most of them and they were Christian men. More time was needed in a more formal way to let them express their experiences and frustrations. One method for this could have been small group discussions and then having someone report out. One of the most enlightening points was seeing the men think about spiritual-mindedness. It was as if some were convicted when realizing they were not thinking of authority from a Christ perspective.

WORKSHOP DATA ANALYSIS

Most of you will probably not be interested in this workshop data analysis section, but may find the focus group discussion analsysis interesting. For this publication, I am not including the statistical analysis and data tables. They are available for review. If a participant did not answer a question, it comes up as a missing variable. Variables are provided for pre and post surveys. All variables that begin with "post" are the variables with the post-test results. A codebook was created for clarity, but not included in this analysis.

The statistics charts show that there are twenty-two responses to all pre survey questions with the exception of mentoring, influence, member, and age. All exceptions had twenty-one responses with the exception of the member variable, which had twenty. The exception means that the participant did not respond to the question.

There are only thirteen valid responses for the post variables. If there were not pre and post responses that matched, the variable is considered missing. Valid post variables needed a pre and post survey that matched by name to measure the level of change. Potential reasons for missing variables include two participants came late and may have not taken the pre-survey. Four participants had to leave early and did not take the post survey. One pre survey did not have a name, therefore it could not be matched to a post survey.

The descriptive statistics tables provide statistics for the number of valid responses (N), the range of scores from the lowest to the highest (range), the lowest score anyone had on that question (minimum), the highest score anyone had on that question (maximum), and the average of all valid scores and the average distance scores were distributed above and below the mean (std. deviation). Some insightful views can be observed from the descriptive statistics that highlight beliefs and perceptions of participants prior to the workshop, as well as after participating in the workshop.

Questions 1–9 allow for responses ranging from 1–5, with the scale as: strongly disagree (1), somewhat agree (2), and strongly agree (5). Participants also have the option of selecting a 3 or a 4. Question one of the pre survey provides the statement "I respect the police." Question two of the pre survey provides the statement, "Police really care about what is good for my neighborhood." The mean for question one (respect) is 3.68 and the mean for question 2 (care) is 2.77. This implies that prior to the workshop, men respected the police more than they believed the police cared about the community. With 5 being the highest possible mean, question 7, "I feel that it is the responsibility of Christian men to educate young Black males on improving police relations" (educate) has the highest mean of all pre survey variables at 4.23. This demonstrates that there is a strong desire for Christian men intervention to improve police relations. The age mean (3.62), places most of the participants in the age range of thirty-six to forty-five years old.

When comparing the pre survey responses to the post survey responses, descriptive statistics show a slight increase in respect for police, willing to assist police, knowledge of scriptures, and knowledge of US history that has influenced Black males' perception of police means. One interesting finding is that there is a slight decrease in the means of the questions about their belief that the police care about what is good for the neighborhood and that most young Black males in the community trust the police. This may be attributed to reviewing the scholarly articles reviewed in the class and hearing the comments from fellow participants.

The post educate variable has the highest mean of 4.7692 and the greatest increase from the corresponding pre survey, supporting the belief that it is the responsibility of Christian men to educate young Black males on improving police relations with a .54 increase. Important to this project, the post mentoring variable had an increase of .791 from the pre mentoring variable, showing an increase in comfort of mentoring young Black males on what specifically to do when they encounter police.

The frequencies charts provide the mean of all valid scores, the median of all scores, and the mode of the most frequently chosen responses. These charts report the educate variable with the highest pre survey mean of 4.23, once again reporting that the participants feel that it is the responsibility of Christian men to educate young Black males on how to improve relationships with police. Strongly agree (5) received the most frequent responses for respect, assist, history, educate, mentoring, and age for the pre survey responses, demonstrating strong common agreement of participants for those responses.

The scriptures variable had the most frequent response of 1 (strongly disagree) on the pre survey, showing that most respondents were not aware of more than five specific biblical scriptures that relate to current Black male police relations. This mode increased to 3 (somewhat agree) on the post survey. The influence mode also increased by two, from 3 to 5, showing an increase in the most common response about participants' awareness of the US history that has influenced Black males' perception of police. Trust was the next most frequent response on the disagree side, with 2 as the mode. This shows that most of the respondents on the pre survey reported that they do not feel that young Black males in the community trust the police. This mode did not change on the post survey. Another difference to highlight is the decline in the mode from 5 to 4 in the pre and post respect question.

What matters most in the frequency table is the valid percent. This tells what percentage of people chose each answer. This only includes the valid responses, those who actually answered the questions. It is acknowledged that there is a relatively low number of valid post responses. Even considering this, interesting, although limited highlights can be observed. The overall findings of this project are strengthened through the utilization of triangulation, gathering common themes from the surveys, small group discussion, and case study.

The first notable highlight in the frequency table is found in the trust variable of the pre survey. Of those responding, 40.9 percent responded with a 2, just one point above strongly disagree, feeling that most young Black males in the community do not trust the police. The lowest percent for this variable is 4.5 for the response of 5, strongly agree. This shows that an overwhelming majority of the participants (77.3) disagreed with the premise that young Black males trust the police prior to participating in the workshop. The next notable highlight is found in the educate pre survey variable, with 22.7 percent responding with a 4 and 54.5 percent responding with a 5. This sum means that 77.2 percent of the participants agree that it is the responsibility of Christian men to educate young Black males on improving police relations. The member variable of the frequency table informs us that 70 percent of the participants were members of the Cup of Salvation Deliverance church. The age variable shows that 28.6 percent of the participants were sixteen to twenty-five years old and the majority of the participants were of the oldest age group, age forty-six and above. The youngest age group, under sixteen, had a representation of 4.8 percent.

Notable post survey responses for the frequency variables table are for post trust, post history, and post mentoring, all at 61.5 valid percent. For the post assist variable, 61.5 percent, or eight of the participants, selected 2, showing that participants disagree with the statement that most young Black males in the community trust the police.

The post trust valid percent of 61.5, reports that eight of the thirteen respondents believed that young Black males do not trust police. The belief that young Black men do not trust the police increased from 40.9 percent (pre workshop) to 61.5 percent for the option of 2 of the level of disagreement. Add that to the 30.8 valid percent of those who responded 1, or strongly disagree, and the total of participants that believe young Black men do not trust the police is twelve out of thirteen post workshop attendees. It is possible that the increase comes due to hearing others provide their opinions and reviewing the articles shared during the workshop.

The post history valid percent of 61.5 reports that eight of the thirteen respondents believed that those participants were aware of the history that has influenced Black males' perceptions of police at the highest option of 5 for strongly agree. The pre history response for the same level of strongly agree was 36.4. This limited comparison shows that participants increased their knowledge on the awareness of US history that has influenced Black males' perceptions of police.

The post mentoring valid percent of 61.5 reports that eight of the thirteen respondents believed they felt comfortable mentoring young Black males about what specifically to do and not to do when they encounter police at the highest option of 5 for strongly agree. This comparative response increased from 38.1 percent on the corresponding pre survey mentoring variable. This limited comparison shows that participants increased their comfort in mentoring.

The highest valid percent of 76.9 (ten of thirteen participants) is associated with the post educate variable, reporting that participants felt that it is the responsibility of Christian men to educate young Black males on improving police relations. This comparative response increased from 54.5 percent on the corresponding pre survey educate variable. This limited comparison shows that participants increased their belief that it is the responsibility of Christian men to educate young Black males on improving police relations.

The paired samples t-test checks the relationships between the responses received on the pre and post test. When looking at previous tables, one can see the differences in the means for the pre and post variables. This lets us know, as reported above, that some of the variable means changed, but do these changes really matter? In some cases, for this project, even modest movement in scores is important. If the workshop can get a person's answers/beliefs to change even a little, it may show that the workshop has value for this historical and sensitive topic.

While any change may provide some level of insight, the paired samples t-test checks to see if there is a "statistically significant difference" between the pre and post scores. This first paired samples t-test table shows the mean for the pre and post for each variable. While similar mean comparisons have already been discussed, this table provides a clear and systemic report. The paired samples statistics table shows several changes in attitude that show the impact of the workshop.

The paired samples test tables are the last two tables. The data is usually reported in one table, but it is split in two to fit on the page. SPSS performs this when the data is exported. The difference in the mean scores has already been reported in the previous paired sample statistics tables. The Mean column of the paired samples test table shows the difference between the means. It prevents the need to calculate the difference in the means. This table allows one to clearly see which variables have the biggest pre and post differences.

The most important column in paired samples test tables is the significance. The very last column on the second part of the table has the "Sig" numbers. For a relationship to be significant, it must be .05 or lower. One can see that the scriptures data is significant and is the only one that is significant. But as one looks at the Mean column, mentoring had the next largest difference after scriptures. It also approaches significance at .056. While it might not be statistically significant according to accepted cutoffs, it is worth reporting.

SUMMARY

The major themes that can be derived from the pre and post surveys are:

Participants feel that Black males do not trust the police, and the workshop increased that belief. Also participants feel it is the responsibility of Christian men to educate young Black males on improving police relations, and this belief increased after the workshop. The participants were not familiar with more than five specific biblical scriptures that relate to current Black male police relations and their familiarity improved after the workshop. After attending the workshop, the participants felt more comfortable about mentoring young Black males specifically on what to do and not to do when they encounter police.

FOCUS GROUP DISCUSSION ANALYSIS

Appendix D contains a transcript of the small group discussion.[151] As a reminder, the purpose of the small group discussion was to evaluate the

---

151 See Appendix D.

workshop. Names were left out of the transcription to maintain the anonymity of the participants. There were a few common themes that came from the small group discussion:

1. A strength of the workshop was the ability to educate the community and Black men about aspects of how to improve police relations and encounters.
2. The workshop provides an opportunity to empower others.
3. Changing Black men's perceptions of police is a potential outcome.
4. Those who attend the workshop should leave with an action plan of next steps.
5. More young men should be included in the workshop.

A few statements not captured in the common themes, but are notable for highlighting include:

1. "We need to first change things within ourselves."
2. "One of the things that this workshop has changed for me is, while I've grown up dealing with a lot of police harassment and was taught how to react to those situations, I can't say that I've taken what I've learned and shared with others…"
3. "I just want to speak on sex offenders and domestic violence…There are common folks getting serious time behind sex offenses. You've got a nineteen-year old sitting in the news, who's got a fourteen- or fifteen-year-old girlfriend. It happens. We just have to stand up as men and educate each other."

Prior to the small group discussion, participants were given a workshop evaluation form to anonymously capture their thoughts.[152] The questions on the workshop evaluation form also guided the small group discussion. This was a method used to capture the thoughts they may not have had the oppor-

---

152 See Appendix D.

tunity to express during the small group discussion, or did not feel comfortable sharing openly with the group. There were four questions on the form:

1. What are the greatest strengths of the workshop?
2. What would you change?
3. Would you recommend the workshop to others? Why or why not?
4. Other comments?

For the question "What are the greatest strengths of the workshop?" the two common themes were:

1. The information learned/increased awareness.
2. The conversation/dialogue that took place.

A few notable comments include:

1. Empowering those who are in need-educating those who are not knowledgeable.
2. The biblical approach to educating black men and fostering improved relations with law enforcement in win-win collaboration opens more dialogue and options.
3. Knowledge of the instructor and statistical data that was introduced.
4. It provided awareness of blacks and police relations. What we can do to promote unity. Informing us on what programs are in place. Open dialogue and challenged thought process.

For the question "What would you change?" seven participants responded that more time was needed for the workshop. Seven of the participants responded that more youth were needed at the workshop. Notable statements from this question include:

1. "Breaking the perceptions that Black males have of police officers, as well as the perceptions that police have of Black males is very important."

2. "Reach out to more pastors and unchurched men to be involved in this ongoing event."
3. "I like the format."
4. "Either increase the duration of the workshop and/or frequency."
5. "Duplicate the format to other churches."
6. "Not just pontificate, but create a real action plan."

For the "Would you recommend the workshop to others?" question, thirteen participants responded yes. Two did not say yes, but implied it in their responses to the "Why, or why not?" question. Those two responses included: Have a proper plan of behavior and response for confronting law enforcement. Check your attitude and tone of voice; and that if you have an encounter with the police, all you have to do is stay calm and be respectful. One participant responded no to recommending the workshop to others. He noted that his friends are below the age requirement.

CASE STUDY

The case study involved an interview with one participant of the workshop who was randomly selected. He is also a member of the church. The open-ended interview was guided by four questions. The transcript is located in Appendix F.[153] Comments that may lead to the identification of the case study participant were deleted to maintain anonymity. The analysis of the interview is broken down into background, development of attitude toward police, workshop strengths, and potential changes to the workshop.

PARTICIPANT BACKGROUND

The participant is an educated Black male who grew up in the Research Triangle Park area. He grew up in a strong Christian home with both parents present. He grew up in an upper lower class community. He has children.

---

153 See Appendix F.

DEVELOPMENT OF ATTITUDE TOWARD POLICE
Participant did not grow up hearing parents speak negatively about police. His father did criticize police after their home was broken into several times and the suspect(s) were not caught. The participant participated in illegal acts in association with peers. He started hearing negative perceptions of police from peers.

WORKSHOP STRENGTHS
The participant "really enjoyed" the workshop and believes that it is needed in the community. He believed that the diversity of Black men's perceptions toward police was uncovered during the conversations, some justified and some unjustified. Hearing from the officer's perspective made him think differently. He believes that young Black men may receive information about understanding and improving police relations from Christian men, using the Reverend Dr. Martin Luther King as a model of trust. Participant liked the section of the workshop that explained why police take certain actions when making vehicle and pedestrian stops and encounters.

RECOMMENDED POTENTIAL CHANGES TO WORKSHOP
1. He would have liked to see uniformed police, more participants, and more participants who were younger.
2. The workshop should have been longer.

NOTABLE STATEMENTS
"Well, I guess from experiences I've had, even though a lot of the men I know are Christians, the older men still have that perception from back in the day of how police treated black men unfairly in the past, and a lot of them just can't get past that. I guess it's that fear or that distrust of police from way back, previous experiences, and they bring it with them, even though now they profess Christ. It's just still like a hurdle that a lot of them just don't get past."

"Just as a man in general, hardworking man, police are hard working men just as I am, and a lot of things they do, they're trying to bring peace to the situations. And you're always going to have some who take it a bit far, but we have to remember that that's not all of them, and it's probably not the majority, but we have to give them the benefit of the doubt that they are here to bring peace, and they're working hard, and may be as fearful as we are in certain situations. I believe that if we can ever get back that unity between black men and police, then a lot of our black men would live longer."

Common Themes from the Interview

1. The workshop was a success.
2. The workshop changed participant's perception of police.
3. The workshop should be duplicated.
4. Young Black men may listen to Christian men.
5. Christian men need to change their perceptions of police.

OVERALL FINDINGS

The findings from the analysis are divided into four categories: relevant information learned, the changes in knowledge and perception of the participants, the value and need for the workshop, and the value of the recommended changes to the workshop. The findings are based on analysis of the data from the pre and post surveys, the small group discussion, and the case study.

RELEVANT INFORMATION LEARNED

1. There are some interesting points (comments) learned from the data that are separate from the evaluation of the intervention. Some of these findings support previous research and/or may serve as a foundation for future research.
2. Black males do not think younger Black males have a positive perception of police.

3. Older Black males' previous experiences with police on an individual level influence their perception of all police and what they communicate to younger Black males.
4. Black males have more confidence in the police than they believe police are concerned about Black communities.
5. Black males' opinions of police are influenced by the opinions of others.

PARTICIPANTS' OPINIONS CHANGED AFTER THE WORKSHOP

1. Prior to the workshop, participants believed that Black males do not trust the police. After hearing data supporting this premise and discussion among themselves, their level of belief in this increased.
2. Prior to the workshop, participants believed that it is the responsibility of Christian men to educate young Black males about how to improve relations with police and that belief increased.
3. The Christian men were not familiar with the five specific biblical scriptures that relate to Black men-police relations and were familiar with more than five after the workshop.
4. Participants had more confidence in their ability to mentor Black males after the workshop.

VALUE OF WORKSHOP

1. The workshop is needed and has value in educating Christian men and strengthening the relationship between young Black males and police.
2. The workshop provides opportunities to empower Black males so when they encounter the police they can proactively engage them.

RECOMMENDED CHANGES TO WORKSHOP
1. The workshop should be longer.
2. More people should attend, especially younger participants.
3. Participants should leave with an action plan and next steps.

It is important to note the lower level of scriptural familiarity. I observed that participants responded from a carnal perspective through the early conversations of the workshop. There was very little reference to Christian spirituality and principles toward the issue of relationships with police. During the first discussion at the Men's Ministry meeting and the first portion of the workshop, men spoke negatively and emotionally about police officers' relationships with the Black community. There was brief silence when the workshop slide presentation introduced the idea of going from carnal minded to spiritual minded. That is, thinking of the issue from a Christ perspective. This single point is what makes this intervention different from other national approaches that address the relationship between Black men and police.

ROUNDTABLE DISCUSSION WITH LAW ENFORCEMENT
During the pre-dissertation defense review, the committee recommended that a roundtable take place allowing dialogue between law enforcement and the sample population to strengthen law enforcement engagement. The premise was that this would aid in improving the perception of law enforcement. I requested permission from Elder Charles Freeman and Executive Pastor Deborah Holloway. There had been a change in the leadership of the Men's Ministry. After approval, e-mails were sent to area law enforcement administrators to participate in the roundtable. The e-mail outlined the purpose of the roundtable.[154] Durham County Sheriff Mike Andrews, Durham Police Department Deputy Chief Larry Smith, and Cary Police Chief Pat Bazemore all responded within an hour that their agencies would participate.

---

154 See Appendix G.

REVEREND DR. MAULIN CHRIS HERRING

On Saturday, November 1, 2014, Cup of Salvation Deliverance Church Men's Ministry and Outstretched Hands Community Development Corporation, Inc. hosted a roundtable discussion focusing on strengthening relationships between Black men and Law Enforcement. Durham Police Department, Durham County Sheriff's Office, and Cary Police Department quickly responded to an invitation to participate. The goal of the roundtable was to provide a forum for intimate conversations about Black males and Law Enforcement relations at the community level.

Thirty-two people attended the roundtable, including one representative of the Durham County Sheriff's Office, three representatives from the Cary Police Department, and two representatives from the City of Durham Police Department. Of the young men and men attending, ten were teenagers or younger. The tables were set up in a rectangle format to ensure eye contact. Outstretched Hands Community Development Corporation, Inc. and members of the Cup Men's Ministry provided breakfast. Elder Freeman opened with a welcome and prayer. A statement was made to law enforcement representatives present that their personal views of religion were respected and they were free to not participate in prayer or they could participate in their personal prayer. The statement recognized that some of the law enforcement personnel were attending on agency time and there was no intent to impose faith upon them. Everyone went around the table introducing themselves. Law enforcement representatives were asked to take a little time to share anything they felt comfortable sharing. Some shared how long they had been in law enforcement, their education, current position, and family information. Several of them had college degrees.

The young men and men attending asked questions about the use of force continuum, law enforcement policies related to vehicle stops, law enforcement interpersonal communication skills and diversity training, and school resource officer practices to name a few. Some of the men and young men also shared what they perceived as negative personal encounters with law enforcement. Law enforcement representatives discussed a number of programs that provide opportunities for the community to get involved with their organizations, including youth-specific programs.

A memorable moment came when a Durham Police Department commanding officer asked "How many of you believe that law enforcement covers up for each other?" The majority immediately raised their hands indicating affirmation. A brief discussion followed about discipline investigation policies. Law enforcement officers stressed the importance of filing a complaint after negative encounters.

All attending were able to learn and experience the personal side of one another. One of the greatest outcomes was the one-on-one conversations that occurred during breaks. The roundtable was scheduled for two hours and lasted two and a half hours. Everyone stressed the importance and need for more conversations of this format.

5

SUMMARY, CONCLUSIONS, RECOMMENDATIONS

WHAT DID I LEARN ABOUT MYSELF DURING THIS STUDY?

First, I learned that I have a more intense and heartfelt passion for the topic than I thought. I came to realize that my commitment and interest in "at risk" Black males and their plight with the criminal justice system that started while I was a rookie police officer at the age of 21 was a foundation that God had laid. This becomes more of a reality considering I only became a police officer because I needed a job. This study also taught me to strengthen my dependency on God when I questioned whether it was worth all the effort. At times, teaching a full course load at a university, managing a national institute, traveling the country facilitating courses, attending to pastoring/ministering responsibilities, and second to my relationship with God, nurturing my family, things seemed overwhelming. That is when I cried out and leaned into God and He always carried me through. I learned that all things are possible as long as you depend on Him and it is of His will.

WHAT DID I LEARN ABOUT THE PEOPLE ASSOCIATED WITH THIS STUDY?

I learned that the men of God who participated in the intervention are Black Christian men who are extremely diverse in their perceptions of Black males and police. While many of them had negative perceptions of police, the degree of resentment and distrust was greatly varying. This showed me that one must be very cautious and not group all Black men together, assuming that their perceptions and attitudes are the same. I also learned that in some cases the resentment toward police was so great and so passionate that these men were willing to abandon their Christian values when discussing their perceptions and experiences about police. I also was reminded that women are extremely interested in the issue and are ready to play a role in addressing the historical problem.

WHAT HAPPENED THAT WAS UNEXPECTED?
I did not expect so many people to embrace the project and my work. Many faculty members at North Carolina Central University were very interested and supportive, even though the degree I was working toward was a Doctor of Ministry as opposed to a Doctor of Philosophy. I did not expect the level of support given by all members at every level of my beloved Cup of Salvation Deliverance Church and Ministries. At times, I was not available and I received expressions of support and understanding. Probably most importantly what was unexpected was the apathy that was expressed when more Christian men from the community did not attend the workshop. Flyers and information were sent to select churches and while many agreed the the topic was important; very few men from other churches attended the workshop. This is similar to what I experienced as a police chief and board member for a "Big Brother" program. It was difficult to get Black men involved during the noncrisis proactive times. I did not expect that to be the case with Christian men.

WHAT WOULD I DO DIFFERENTLY?
First and most importantly, I would set aside more prayer time intensely seeking God's voice. At times I needed to be more in tune to when to say yes and when to say no when others asked for my assistance and help on projects. I would make the workshop a full day and include more churches in the

process. This would mean collaboration with pastors and men's ministries to ensure the sermons and Bible teachings also took place. I would also include Christian law enforcement officers in the intervention.

POTENTIAL NEXT STEPS FOR YOUR CHURCH

There are a number of options that Chrisian organizations can consider to address the problem, based on this study. First, acknowledge that the problem is big, historic and complex enough that it will take the intervention of the Holy Spirit to bring about change. Christians must not rely on their emotions.

WORKSHOPS WITH CHRISTIANS

One option is to host a series of long-term strategically planed workshops that Spiritually prepare all members of the church to mentor and educate members of the community on what to do when approached by law enforcement, how to get proactively involved with local law enforcement and the importance on getting involved with local council and commissioner meetings. All of this must be taught from a spiritual minded perspective. The first series of workshops should focus on Chrisitan doctrine, without local law enforcement present, to spiritually prepare the participants. It may be benefical to have Chrisitan law enforcement represetatives present, if known.

WORKSHOPS WITH LAW ENFORCEMENT

A series of workshops can be held with law enforcement. The benefits can be great, providing opportunity for law enforcement to hear from the Chrisitan community and allowing the Chrisitan community to hear from law enforcement. Negative and positive shared experiences can be greatly beneficial. It is important to have the appropriate facilitator who will allow for open expression, without allowing shouting and anger. During these sessions in the past, I have often had Black men state that they have never had the opportunity to have personal and in depth conversations with law enforcement.

PRAYER AND BIBLE STUDY

Antoher option is for ecclesiastical staff to develop a series of sermons and bible studies to provide biblical insight of the situation. Dealing with an oppressive authority is clearly addressed throughout the bible. Ecclesiatical staff must also stand fast in the belief and power of prayer, organizing corporate prayer strategies within their church, as well as bring other churches together. This should not be the traditional coming-together for a prayer session, but rather, well thought out and developed strategic plans.

LOCAL LAW ENFORCEMENT AND COMMUNITY ENGAGEMENT

The church should identify ways to prayerfully and proactively engage local law enforcement. They should deteremine what initiatives exist and consider collaboration to develop programs if they do not exist. Often programs sponsored by law enforcement exist, but members of the Black community do not make the time to participate. Some of the initiatives include:

- Citizen Police Academies
- Community Meetings To Address (solve) Specific Problems
- Ride Along Programs
- Police Athletic Leagues
- Citizen Advisory Boards
- Citizen Participation in Officer Hiring and Promotion

The more time local law enforcement and community spend together, the more trust and understanding is developed. That not only can lessen negative encounters, it can develop partnerships that lead to crime reduction and more safe communities.

LAW ENFORCMENT ORGANIZATIONAL TRANSFORMATION AND STRATEGIC COMMUNITY ENGAGEMENT

Leadership in the Christian community may choose to become more educated on measures that local law enforcement should consider in assessing and improving policy and organizational structure. There are systemic organizational challenges that often law enforcement management does not have the knowledge, resources, or support to address. Some of these measures may include:

- a true understanding of community oriented policing as a management style
- hiring and selection policy assessment
- early warning systems
- strategic community problem solving
- complaint tracking systems

As the Christian community leadership become more knowledgeable in some of these areas, they may even serve as a resource to law enforcement management in geting buy-in from law enforcement employees and support from poltical leaders for funding.

EX-OFFENDER COMMUNITY RE-ENTRY

Another approach that some churches may want to take is assisting those who have been incarcerated, or who have arrest records. It is often difficult for ex-offenders to overcome the stigma of serving time, or having arrest records. They often need help with finding employment, education, training and mental health support that will allow them to live successful and productive lives. This is truly a population that Christ would have assisted; the many in the community who have been rejected by others.

CONCLUSION

While this project focused on changing the perceptions and actions of young Black males by educating Christian men to foster that change, work needs to continue to change the perceptions and actions of police toward Black males. Michael Birzer (2008) interviewed Black males about their perception of police. His research findings document the qualities that Black males think police officers need to execute and possess to consider the contact positive. The human relations traits expressed by the Black males participating in his research are cultural sensitivity, empathy, and fairness. Further research is needed to explore why even though police receive training to gain these characteristics identified by Birzer, some in law enforcement do not demonstrate these characteristics and Blacks continue to have more negative perceptions of police when compared to Whites. More research and intervention needs to take place addressing police officers' perceptions of Black males and what impact those perceptions have during encounters. The model and workshop developed and tested for this project needs to be replicated using more time for the workshop and a larger population of participants.

APPENDICES

APPENDIX A

SERMON: MOSES AND THE PLIGHT OF YOUNG BLACK MEN IN THE UNITED STATES AND AUTHORITY

Pastor M. Chris Herring
November 2013
Cup of Salvation Deliverance Church and Ministries

To fix a problem, a sickness, or a plague, it is necessary to identify the problem. Once the specific problem is confirmed, it is necessary to come up with a solution, an intervention to the problem. It takes the right, skilled person(s) to carry out the intervention. Sometimes they have studied for years and sometimes they are just gifted for the intervention. To address a problem, you must be willing to acknowledge the problem.

Examples: high blood pressure; my rotator cuff injury; cancer; a vehicle starter; Freon in an air conditioning unit; split ends.

The problem will exist, or often get worse, until the problem has been diagnosed, a solution identified, and intervention takes place.

Read selected statistics of Black men in America (crime, education, employment).

Story of Moses:

Read scriptures in narrative format:

Genesis
    45:24–28
    46:2–6
    47:1–7
    Exodus
    1:6–10
    1:16–17
    1:22
    2:3
    2:5–6
    2:10–12
    2:14–16
    2:19
    2:21
    2:23
    3:3
    3:9–10

Moses was a killer. He committed murder. He did wrong when he was a young man and he ran from authority. Even though he did wrong as a young man, God had a plan for him. He was taken in and nurtured. When the time was right, God called him up to do a great and mighty thing, to deliver Israel out of bondage.

The Book of the Covenant (Exodus 20:22)

Moses wrote "all the words of the Lord." (Exodus 24:4)

The Ten Commandments (Exodus 34:4 and 27–29)

African American Men and the Police

The law of the Lord (Luke 2:22 and 2:30)

God used both the educational system of Egypt and Moses's exile in Midian to prepare Moses to represent his people before a powerful Pharaoh and to guide his people out of exile through the wilderness.

There are many Black men who have done wrong, maybe even served time in jail and now have accepted Jesus Christ as their Lord and Savior. They can serve as excellent resources to leading young Black men out of the clutches of the criminal justice system.

There are many young Black men who have done wrong, but who still have much to offer. There is a plan for their lives if someone steps in and intervention takes place.

The criminal justice system has turned out to be an oppressor of young Black men. The question is why and what is the solution? Who is the solution?

It is extremely important to acknowledge that the unjust practices and acts of the criminal justice system and law enforcement must be addressed. Change must come. Who better to bring about that needed change than Black men, young Black men?

Black men must see themselves as the needed change agents to fix the problem.

We must move from a carnal way of thinking to a Spiritual way of thinking to eliminate the plague.

Has the power of the Holy Ghost truly been called on to fix historic conflict between African American men and law enforcement?

Black young men must have an Exodus from the mentality that police are their enemy. Black young men must have an Exodus from the mentality that it is an "us against them" world. Deliverers are needed. Exodus is a departure, it is an exit.

There is a need for an Exodus from the mentality that no one cares and the only way out is the illegal way, or violent way.

I'm not saying to trust the police and that the police are always right, but rather young men should not let a mentality toward anyone hold back and control their destiny and the community's destiny.

Yes, law enforcement must be held accountable, without question. There should also be acknowledgment that things have changed and the "us versus them" mentality must change. There are avenues in place to address an unjust and oppressive criminal justice system.

There are several national professional organizations that focus on issues related to the Black community like the National Association of Blacks in Criminal Jutstice. There are professional organizations in just about every state that support issues related to Black law enforcement officers like North State of North Carolina. There is the National Organization of Black Law Enforcement Executives located near Washington, DC. On the prosecution side, there is the Black Bar Association. There are many Black judges who have an understanding of the challenges of the Black community Judge Elaine Oneal Bushfan, here in Durham, NC.

Do not tell me things have not changed; they have. It is a new day. Now we must seize the opportunity and change our mentality. The Israelites after the Exodus still had a slave mentality, not believing in what they had seen and what they had been told.

While much has changed, it seems as if young Black males continue to be oppressed, for some, the oppression is self-inflicted.

The statistics and research confirm the problem. The question is; what is the intervention? Who is the intervention? Who is the solution?

God has made it very clear to me that his disciples of today, those who have answered the call, are the solution. Christians have the power to intervene and deliver young Black men from what seems to be decades of oppression.

All have a role, White, Black, and Hispanic…the evidence is there. The plague is contagious, young females and Latinos also seem to be catching the sickness.

There are some young Black males who are mentally oppressed believing that **all** police, society, and the **entire** system are against them. It makes them react and act with a slave mentality rather than a mentality that this is **their** police department, **their** government, and **their** society. It seems as if some **do not believe** they have the opportunity to achieve. There needs to be an Exodus, a deliverance of their attitude and their beliefs. Christians are their deliverers. More to the point, Christian men can be their Moses.

The question is; are we willing to intervene, or wait until the next media tragedy and gossip about it? Are we willing to intervene or look at the "Black on Black" and "Hispanic on Hispanic" homicide rate and work on protecting our own (family) rather than intervening, hoping our own do not become victimized?

As Christians, we can intervene, if we see ourselves as the solution. Imagine if young Black males changed their attitudes toward police and saw them as friends, rather than foes; seeing the police as working for them, rather than against them. Imagine if young Black males had an attitude that *I can partner with police to strengthen my community.* If God can part the Red Sea and deliver a people out of oppression, He can deliver young Black men from the arms of the criminal justice system.

Christians are the Moseses of today. An exodus and deliverance is without question possible. Even those who have done wrong can be used, if they submit to the will of God. Like Moses, I may not see the Promised Land, a reduction in the statistics, but I will do what God has called me to do.

Matthew 19:26 - But Jesus beheld [them], and said unto them, With men this is impossible; but with God all things are possible.

Luke 1:37 - For with God nothing shall be impossible.

Philippians 4:13 - I can do all things through Christ which strengtheneth me.

Mark 10:27 - And Jesus looking upon them saith, With men [it is] impossible, but not with God: for with God all things are possible.

Mark 9:23 - Jesus said unto him, If thou canst believe, all things [are] possible to him that believeth.

Matthew 17:20 - And Jesus said unto them, Because of your unbelief: for verily I say unto you, If ye have faith as a grain of mustard seed, ye shall say unto this mountain, Remove hence to yonder place; and it shall remove; and nothing shall be impossible unto you.

The change must begin with the people of God, who have the power of the Holy Spirit, to use the teachings of Christ and finally fix the problem, the sickness, the plague!

Appendix B

CSDC BIBLE STUDY 10/25/13

Lazarus Territory and Outstretched Hands

Associate Pastor M. Chris Herring
maulinherring@yahoo.com

From the Vision and Mission Statement
...CSDC is *evangelistically oriented* in that our mission to **"Reach Them, Teach Them, and Set Them Free"** is designed to accomplish the *Great Commission* as directed by Jesus himself. We are committed to winning back our region for God.

As such, we have carved out a neighboring territory for which we claim total spiritual accountability and named it the Lazarus Territory. We will win that territory for God as our Jerusalem Mission. We have also attached ourselves to other likeminded churches to win back the *Research Triangle Area* for God as our Judea Mission. To date, we have established the first of many *outpost ministries* in Kisii, Kenya (Cup of Salvation Kenya) as our Uttermost Parts of the Earth Mission. We are very serious about evangelism.

Lazarus Territory Boundary Points
Hoover Road Apartments
1126 Hoover Road
Durham, NC 27703

YE Smith Elementary Museum School
2410 East Main St.
Durham, NC 27703

Southern High School
800 Clayton Road
Durham, NC 27703

Neal Middle School
201 Baptist Rd
Durham, NC 27704

Cup of Salvation Deliverance Church and Ministries
70 Parkside Plaza, 1020 Highway 70 East
Durham, NC 27703

Census Data From 2010 Zip Code 27703 Basic Demographics
Population: 43,622
Hispanic (of all races): 7,654
Not Hispanic by Race:
White: 11,824
Black or African American: 22,158
Native American: 147
Asian: 988
Pacific Islander: 8
Other race: 111
Multirace: 732

Housing units: 12,625
Owner-occupied housing units: 4,557
Renter-occupied housing units: 7,224
School-aged population (5–17 years of age): 6,223
Population 65 years of age or older: 2,521

Hoover Road Apartments
1126 Hoover Road **Community Type** Conventional Public Housing Durham, NC 27703

About This Community
Hoover Road was completed in 1968 and is comprised of fifty-four multifamily townhouse apartments. The community is located in East Durham.

- **Review statistics on poor academic achievement rates by race.**
- **Review crime statistics by race.**

APPENDIX C

WORKSHOP ANNOUNCEMENT FLYER

African American Men and The Police: A Christ Solution for the New Millennium

While people of color make up about 30 percent of the United States' population, they account for 60 percent of those imprisoned.

According to the Bureau of Justice Statistics, one in three black men can expect to go to prison during their lifetime.

According to the US Department of Education, African American students are arrested far more often than their white classmates.

Voter laws that prohibit people with felony convictions to vote disproportionately impact men of color according to the Center for American Progress

Historically, African American men and police have had a relationship of oppression, racism, and strain. This relationship has created negative perceptions of police and the criminal justice system among many African American males. While the issues are complex, Jesus has the solution. Cup of Salvation Men's Ministry and Outstretched Hands Community Development

Corporation are sponsoring *African American Men and The Police: A Christ Solution for the New Millennium.*

Who: Men 16 years old and older
When: February 1, 2014 (Saturday)
Time: 9:30 a.m. to 1:00 p.m.
Location: Cup of Salvation Deliverance Church and Ministries CUP Center
1020 Highway 70 East, P.O. Box 11617, Durham, NC 27703

Pastor M. Chris Herring will serve as facilitator. Pastor Herring has more than 32 years of experience in the criminal justice field and served as the first Black chief of police for two communities. He initiated a number of programs strengthening relationships between the Black and Hispanic communities and the police. Herring has worked with hundreds of at risk young men in communities throughout the United States, helping start programs that focused on vulnerable youth.

A light breakfast will be provided and special drawings for those attending the full workshop will take place. Please confirm your attendance by January 24 as seating is limited.

APPENDIX D

WORKSHOP HANDOUTS

WORKSHOP AGENDA
African American Men and The Police: A Christ Solution for the New Millennium

9:30 to 9:50   Welcome
Prayer
Praise and worship
Introductions
Pre survey

9:50 to 10:15   Foundation scriptures
Personal experiences of police interactions (brief discussion)
Benefits of improved black male police relationships
     Improved perceptions of police
     Knowledge of what to do during police encounters
     Influencing police operations
Destiny Denied: Black Man's Prevention and Survival Guide To Police Encounters

10:15 to 10:30	Biblical scriptures that bring insight into police relations
10:30 to 10:40	Why are we here? Statistics tell the story
10:40 to 10:50	Break
10:50 to 11:00	External influences of perceptions of police Where do black men get their perception of police? Brief historical overview of black male/police relations
11:00 to 11:10	Advances of blacks in the criminal justice system
11:10 to 11:30	Mentoring young black males about relationships with police
11:30 to 11:40	Police officer diversity
11:40 to 12:10	What to do during police encounters
12:10 to 12:20	Influencing police departments
12:20 to 12:30	Post survey; closing remarks; prayer
12:30 to 12:55	Small group discussion: workshop evaluation What did you find most helpful? What did you find the least helpful? Do you feel more empowered? What would you change? Would you recommend the workshop to others?
12:55 to 1:00	Gift Card Drawing/Closing Prayer

CONSENT FORM

CONSENT TO PARTICIPATE IN RESEARCH

African American Men and The Police: A Christ Solution for the New Millennium Program Study

You are invited to participate in a research study conducted by Maulin Chris Herring, who is a doctoral student from the Doctor of Ministry program at Apex School of Theology. Mr. Herring is conducting this study for his doctoral research project. Dr. Artist McKinley Royal is his faculty mentor for this project.

Your participation in this study is entirely voluntary. You should read the information below and ask questions about anything you do not understand before deciding whether or not to participate. You are being asked to participate in this study because you have an interest in the relationship between Black males and police.

- **PURPOSE OF THE STUDY**

The purpose of this study is to develop a workshop that will equip and motivate men, using Christian principles, to mentor young Black men on how to improve their perceptions of police. You do not have to be a Christian or be affiliated with a church to participate in the study. We hope to use what we learn from the study to strengthen relationships between young Black men and police.

- **PROCEDURES**

If you volunteer to participate in this study, we will ask you to do the following:

1. Participate in a two-hour workshop.
2. Complete pre and post workshop questionnaires. You will be asked to provide your name.

3. Participate in a small group discussion to evaluate the workshop. This session will be audio recorded.
4. Complete a brief anonymous written evaluation of the workshop.

- **POTENTIAL RISKS AND DISCOMFORTS**

We expect that any risks, discomforts, or inconveniences will be minor and we believe they are not likely to happen. If discomfort becomes a problem, you may discontinue your participation.

- **POTENTIAL BENEFITS TO SUBJECTS AND/OR TO SOCIETY**

You may benefit from the study by changing your perception of and strengthening your preparedness to mentor men on how to improve their relationships with police. You may also gain information on what to do when one encounters police. The research has potential in reducing the rates of arrests and incarcerations of Black males in America. The research also has the potential in reducing crime rates in neighborhoods.

- **COMPENSATION FOR PARTICIPATION**

You will not receive any payment or compensation for participation in this study. There is also no cost to you for participation. A random drawing of a gift card from the names of those who participate in the full study will take place at the end of the day.

- **CONFIDENTIALITY**

Any information obtained in connection with this study and that can be identified with you will remain confidential and will be disclosed only with your permission. We will not use your name in any of the information we get from this study or in any of the research reports. When the study is finished, we will destroy the list that shows your name.

REVEREND DR. MAULIN CHRIS HERRING

Information that can identify you individually will not be released to anyone outside the study. Mr. Herring will, however, use the information collected in his research project and other publications. We also may use any information that we get from this study in any way we think is best for publication or education. Any information we use for publication will not identify you individually.

The audio recordings we make will not be heard by anyone outside the study unless we have you sign a separate permission form allowing us to use them. The recordings will be destroyed three years after the end of the study, as required by the funding organization.

Pictures may be taken and used on the Outstretched Hand CDC website. If you do not want your picture to be used, please advise Mr. Herring.

I understand the procedures described above. My questions have been answered to my satisfaction, and I agree to participate in this study.

_____

Printed Name of Subject

_____   _____

Signature of Subject   Date

PRE/POST SURVEYS

NAME: _____

PRE SURVEY

1. **I respect the police.**
   Strongly Disagree *Somewhat Agree* *Strongly Agree*
   1 *2* *3* *4* *5*

2. **Police really care about what is good for my neighborhood.**
   Strongly Disagree *Somewhat Agree* *Strongly Agree*
   1 *2* *3* *4* *5*

3. **I would assist a police officer if he/she needed help.**
   Strongly Disagree *Somewhat Agree* *Strongly Agree*
   1 *2* *3* *4* *5*

4. **I feel that most young Black males in the community trust the police.**
   Strongly Disagree *Somewhat Agree* *Strongly Agree*
   1 *2* *3* *4* *5*

5. **I am aware of more than five specific biblical scriptures that address current Black male-police relations.**
   Strongly Disagree *Somewhat Agree* *Strongly Agree*
   1 *2* *3* *4* *5*

6. **I am aware of the US history that has influenced Black males' perception of police.**
   Strongly Disagree *Somewhat Agree* *Strongly Agree*
   1 *2* *3* *4* *5*

7. I feel it is the responsibility of Christian men to educate young Black males about how to improve police relations.
   Strongly Disagree　　　　*Somewhat Agree*　　　　*Strongly Agree*
   　　1　　　　*2*　　　　*3*　　　　*4*　　　　*5*

8. I feel comfortable mentoring young Black males about specific things to do and not do when they encounter police.
   Strongly Disagree　　　　*Somewhat Agree*　　　　*Strongly Agree*
   　　1　　　　*2*　　　　*3*　　　　*4*　　　　*5*

9. I am aware of actions I can take that will positively influence police operations when it comes to the Black community.
   Strongly Disagree　　　　*Somewhat Agree*　　　　*Strongly Agree*
   　　1　　　　*2*　　　　*3*　　　　*4*　　　　*5*

10. I am a member of Cup of Salvation Deliverance Church.
    a. Yes　　　　b. No

11. I fall into the following age group:
    a. Under 16
    b. 16–25
    c. 26–35
    d. 36–45
    e. 46 and above

NAME: _____

POST SURVEY

1. I am aware of the US history that has influenced Black males' perception of police.
   Strongly Disagree   Somewhat Agree   Strongly Agree
   1   2   3   4   5

2. I feel comfortable mentoring young Black males about specific things to do and not to do when they encounter police.
   Strongly Disagree   Somewhat Agree   Strongly Agree
   1   2   3   4   5

3. I feel that most young Black males in the community trust the police.
   Strongly Disagree   Somewhat Agree   Strongly Agree
   1   2   3   4   5

4. Police really care about what is good for my neighborhood.
   Strongly Disagree   Somewhat Agree   Strongly Agree
   1   2   3   4   5

5. I am aware of more than five specific biblical scriptures that address current Black male police relations.
   Strongly Disagree   Somewhat Agree   Strongly Agree
   1   2   3   4   5

6. I respect the police.
   Strongly Disagree   Somewhat Agree   Strongly Agree
   1   2   3   4   5

7. **I feel it is the responsibility of Christian men to educate young Black males about how to improve police relations.**

   Strongly Disagree　　　　*Somewhat Agree*　　　　*Strongly Agree*
   　　　1　　　　2　　　　3　　　　4　　　　5

8. **I am aware of actions I can take that will positively influence police operations when it comes to the Black community.**

   Strongly Disagree　　　　*Somewhat Agree*　　　　*Strongly Agree*
   　　　1　　　　2　　　　3　　　　4　　　　5

9. **I would assist a police officer if he/she needed help.**

   Strongly Disagree　　　　*Somewhat Agree*　　　　*Strongly Agree*
   　　　1　　　　2　　　　3　　　　4　　　　5

ROBBINS'S CHRISTIAN AUTHORITY ARTICLE

VL-102
Unless otherwise stated, all scripture references were taken from The New King James Bible, © Thomas Nelson Inc., 1982.
© Dale A. Robbins, 1994
Victorious Publications
www.victorious.org
By Dr. Dale A. Robbins
What Every Christian Should Know about Authority

***

Welch's *Black Male Stereotypes and Racial Profiling* Article

BLACK CRIMINAL STEREOTYPES AND RACIAL PROFILING
Kelly Welch
Villanova University, Pennsylvania
http://www.sagepub.com/gabbidonstudy/articles/Welch.pdf

Journal of Contemporary Criminal Justice
Volume 23 Number 3
August 2007 276–288. © 2007 Sage Publications

WORKSHOP EVALUATION (SMALL GROUP SESSION)

WORKSHOP EVALUATION

****You do NOT have to give your name. Responses are anonymous.****

- What are the greatest strengths of the workshop?

- What would you change?

- Would you recommend this workshop to others? Why or why not?

- Other comments?

APPENDIX E

SMALL GROUP TRANSCRIPTION

Herring: Here's what we want to do. I want to hear your comments on the workshop and we'll start off on the question of what are the greatest strengths of the workshop? And it can be something you wrote down, what you didn't, but I just need some feedback. And you can see there are other things that will come up. You can say anything. I'm just trying to lead us.

Participant: Having the ability to empower those in the community to become educated, to be able to make a difference in the community. To want to stand up and start learning a way to give back positively. Being able to educate those that are not informed. Inform those that are less fortunate. Take what we can from this and be willing in a positive way to educate our young black men.

Herring: Any other benefits?

Participant: The collaboration is a mastermind concept where everybody has individual thought processes but out of the collaboration there can be fifteen people in the room, but there can be a sixteenth or seventeenth mind due to the collaboration so we actually have real solutions that we can actually implement and create an action plan and do as opposed to just talking about it. Now we're empowered so that we can actually go out and take action.

Herring: Anything else on the greatest strengths of the workshop?

Participant: I like that it forces you to rethink what you think you know that causes you to look at things differently and try to see things from a different perspective.

Participant: The discussion sparked very useful information. It gives you introspective to reflect on, whether it was from experiences past and present from a historical standpoint. The discussion was stimulating and phenomenal in my opinion.

Participant: (*inaudible*) I think that the community hopes and that we will continue to push. But we hope that it can be changed and that we can change those perceptions in a positive way.

Herring: What would you change? What's wrong? What needs to be changed?

Participant: This was a great workshop. I appreciate the opinions and thoughts and all of the insights, but I would prefer to have a younger audience. I'm forty-three and I would get some younger guys here, but not just for the younger audience, but an audience that is not as established as (specific name given) young brother. Have a focus. Bro. (specific name) was a good brother, as you said, insightful, but I would rather have a group of younger brothers so that we could really see what is going on. We have our experiences and I have my experiences as well, but I would rather have a mass group of young people so that we can really converse with these young men and at least get it out there.

Herring: I want to hear what's changed. Remembering too, and I hope you'll talk about the next phase or steps, that one of the reasons for this is, can we at least start Christian men with carrying the conversation forward. From the perspective of changing the paradigm shift of Christian men and then going forth (that's the focus here), give me more on that. What are the strengths or challenges when it becomes an argumentative debate? That's going to come because there's so much emotion. What do you do with that? If it was about this community and we brought police officers in here, it then becomes about the police, sometimes. I guess I'm trying to find out if you see what I'm trying to do, and then figure out if I'm off on that.

Participant: So the panel *(inaudible)* and you have in this community the church, put a couple of the pastors on the panel, put someone from the community on the panel where they can speak from each perspective. That way it will cover the spiritual perspective, from inside the community perspective, from the police perspective, from the person that's being approached perspective. Someone who can be considered an expert in that field.

Participant: One of the things I would add is duration and/or frequency, but also some definitive action steps, some take-aways, so we're not just meeting and talking about it, because that's what happens. We do that. We pontificate about it all day long, but when the rubber meets the road, we should leave here with not just a question about what we're going to do, but even if there's just one thing that we can go do, we can go do it and be held accountable for it so the next time we meet, we can say this is what I did, this is what we did so that we can have some measurable, quantifiable actions.

Herring: Here's the question I want to ask with that. Would brothers have come out if it were longer, and how do we get them out? And we'll come back to that, but think about it…would brothers come out if it were longer (because we were kinda challenged coming in here this morning ourselves), so how do you get more time, and what we've seen a lot in the community is how do you get brothers to commit to the next step?

Participant: I just wanted to say one thing. There are changes that we need to look at. We need to first change things within ourselves. Now myself personally, being retired from the military, I know one person here that I have known about three years, and every time I have had the opportunity to think that I was giving him the right direction or right positive information, I have always done that. I try to give him my history and everything I can to see and allow him to know. You have to learn to want to give back. You have to empower those who want to be empowered, but most of all, you have to take these challenges and go with it. Don't let anybody stop you in that process, whatever it is. Always remember that if there's an opportunity for you to give back, just remember where you came from. And if (young person's name) can remember that. I try to give him as much information as I can. So I didn't just start today. I started years ago.

Herring: So that whole concept of the mentoring.

Participant: If we really want to get something done, we've got to take on the gangbangers in town. I've dealt with a lot of gangbangers in town, and you know what I found out? They are the only people who are willing to die for what they believe in. They are ordinary people just like us, but they're misdirected. We need an action plan. If we can get gangbangers in this organization…if we can get them straightened out, they're going in the wrong direction…we need to get them in the right direction. They're not scared of the mayor. They're not scared of city hall. Whatever mission you give to them and they can see the vision, they will execute it because they have something that we don't have as Christian men. They are not afraid.

Herring: I want to get about three more. Y'all need to help me. (Calls up participants to demonstrate.) Here's my experience with gangbangers. I could tell you about some recent experiences. He's in his neighborhood and somebody jumps on him. He gets a bad beating. No money, no this, challenges, sees all the other stuff, gets a bad butt-beating, he's just trying to walk home. He (points to someone else) can offer him protection. He (points to someone else) can offer him money. He (points to someone else) can offer him peace. He doesn't want to, but decides to come over here (join gang) because of all of that stuff. So the question, if and when we see this in church, (*come here*), where's the block? Where's the person in between the two? Often when it comes to the gangbangers early on, black men aren't there. Not always, but it happens.

Herring: Give me about three more. What else would you change? Or any comments about the workshop at all.

Participant: I like the myth busters like the rest of what you talked about with the ID…why the police do what they do. Because sometimes if I have an idea of something has to happen to me, then I may be able to better deal with it. Like, if you take money out of my paycheck and I know where it's going, then I can deal with it. And so knowing why they do what they do is a help.

Herring: Any other comments?

Participant: One of the things that this workshop has changed for me is, while I've grown up, dealing with a lot of police harassment, but I was taught how to react in those situations. I can't say that I've taken what I've learned and shared that with others. So what I'm receiving now is the responsibility that we have as men and young men in our community. The information that we have received, to begin to share that with others to empower others, but also, I didn't even know that all of these programs were out there. I had no idea. So for me, that's very enlightening.

Herring: Good. Good. Thank you.

Participant: I just want to speak on sex offenders and domestic violence. We just have to stand up as men. They are really, really sensitive subjects, but we're losing those two groups of folk—men that we focused on—the gangbangers. They're common folks getting serious time behind sex offenses. You've got a nineteen-year-old sitting in the news, who's got a fourteen- or fifteen-year-old girlfriend. It happens. We just have to stand up as men educate each other. We just have to be men. Our friends, family, neighbors. It's all right if you don't know somebody, but sometimes we have to step in and say, hey.

Herring: I love Bro. ##### passion because part of the system he's been in. And remember this is just one workshop that we're trying to get that can be modeled as a beginning.

Participant: This is consistent with domestic violence. If I see something a lot of times, anything else, if I see somebody sagging, I won't say something because you can't talk to everybody if they're not in your circle because there's going to be a conflict. But when it comes to domestic violence I gotta say something.

Herring: I love it, I love it. All right, brothers, I do want to close out in prayer. Min. #####, I'm going to ask you to close out in a strong prayer because of what this is about. I appreciate you, love you, and I will let you know how this continues and goes. Thank you for coming out.

Participant: Let us pray. Heavenly Father, we give you all glory, honor, and praise on this day, Father. I thank you, Lord, for this informational session, this workshop. Lord God you brought all of these wonderful black men together that we might begin to learn about the relations of our inner-city communities, out black community, and police officers, Lord. I thank you for the information that was shared, I thank you for the dialogue, Lord I'm thankful for the words of wisdom that were poured into each person of how to do more to go out and inform one another in the community, Lord God. Father I thank you for your word, Lord, and how we see that we are to abide by the law, but understanding that the law that you have given us, the law of love and of forgiveness, and of being informed and educated to know how to make the right decisions according to your will. We ask, Father, that as we go out, that we will not just go out and take this information and package it and put it away, but that we will take what we have learned today, and even if we only share it with one person, Father God, that we will begin to be that true ambassador of Christ and that we are truly impacting our community as we go forth. So Father, we ask that you continue to have your way in our lives, Lord God. I thank you for Pastor Herring, Lord God, and putting this information together, for setting up this workshop, for stepping out on faith, Lord God, to make an impact, to make a change. I thank you for all of the brothers that are in here, whether they are over certain programs, or they're nonprofits or for-profit, entrepreneurialism, working on a job day in and day out, that wherever we go, knowing that we are working in your field, Lord God, that we are enhancing the kingdom of God as we go forth, empowering others to know you in the power of your resurrection. Lord we ask that you continue to have your way. In Jesus's name we pray, Amen.

APPENDIX F

CASE STUDY INTERVIEW TRANSCRIPTION

Herring: Your identity will remain confidential. The information will be used as part of a Doctorate of Ministry research project for Apex School of Theology. You are free to stop answering questions at any time. Do you understand and agree to participate in the study?

Participant: Yes.

Herring: I just have a series of questions that I want to ask you just to guide the discussions. Anything that you want to add or however you go with it is fine. I just want the guide. To begin with, what is your age and ethnicity?

Participant: My age is (thirties), and I am African American.

Herring: And your gender is…

Participant: Male.

Herring: I want to make sure that with that deep voice, that doesn't mean everything. So now share briefly a little bit about your childhood, you know, growing up, as an example, the city, number of parents in the home, type of neighborhood, just share with us a little bit about that.

Participant: OK. I had both my parents growing up. Both parents were Christians. We grew up Christian upbringing. I had a really great childhood. They really took good care of us. Wasn't very wealthy, but they made sure we had everything we needed and more. My parents were really great at giving to others. They really showed us how to show love and help the community as far as helping with rent and needs, and just giving as much as they could.

Herring: Excellent. Excellent. Did you attend college?

Participant: I did attend college.

Herring: Excellent. Now I just want to switch a little bit and go back to your childhood and family and things like that as you were growing up. What types of conversations did you hear in your home, if any, about police?

Participant: Well, we really didn't hear much about police. Didn't have much interaction with the police. Only a couple of times when our home was burglarized. There was one point in time when it was burglarized about three times back to back and that raised a few eyebrows because after the second time, I could tell that they were a little upset, thinking that more could be done. But our community was [not] the best community. We were in houses, but we were in a low income housing area, but other than that, there were not a lot of dealings with police, except for when my father would try to help at-risk men and would talk to the police for the men and try to keep them out of jail and out of trouble. But that was pretty much all of our dealings with the police.

Herring: Now if you will reflect back, then, and, considering that, what is the earliest age that you can think of that you started having some type of view or perspective of police?

Participant: When I started developing a view of the police, I think that started with my group of friends. Once I got old enough to actually hang out in the neighborhood unsupervised, some of my friends didn't have the same kind of morals or upbringing that I did so they would do some things that were against the law, and my being with them would bring me down with them as well, such as stealing out of the store and tearing things up in the store, ripping packages, so we would get stopped by the police or undercover cop. And then, seeing how they interacted with the police started to get me to see that, OK, that we should be against the police. But that would be the first time that I would have any kind of negative views toward the police.

Herring: And if you care to share, just know that this is confidential, have you participated in any illegal activities yourself? Anything that you would just like to share?

Participant: I have. I kind of began to hang out in the streets a lot and began to dibble and dabble in things that I shouldn't have as far as alcohol and hanging with the wrong crowd, which then I began to do as they did. So yes, I did have a point of time in which I did do things that were against the law.

Herring: Now let's switch hats here a little bit. I know that you attended the *African American Men and the Police: A Christ Solution for the New Millennium* workshop that I facilitated. What were your thoughts about the workshop?

Participant: I really enjoyed the workshop and I think that it's something that is really needed in our community because of the conversation that came up and the different viewpoints, just seeing how scattered men are with our perceptions of police, being justified or unjustified. In our own minds, it seems we all just have so many opinions about the police, but what this conference showed me is that a lot of times, we don't give the police the benefit of the doubt and we never stop to look at it from their point of view. So having heard from a different perspective, maybe from the policeman's point of view really helped me to see that, wow, I should've done a whole lot of things differently and I think that if that message is spread out more, then a whole lot more of other young men would start thinking differently with their actions and interactions with the police.

Herring: Let's take that to another level where you're saying that if that information was shared. Let's now move that to if that information was shared from Christian men to even young boys who are not Christians, or it was coming from Christian men to speak to other young men about mentoring relationships. So, do you think the concept of Christian men mentoring young black men to strengthen police relationships, is a workable or a good concept?

Participant: I think that it is, and the reason why I think it is because, at one point in time, they have been told about great men like Dr. Martin Luther King who was introduced as a strong Christian man who stood up for our rights, and I think just that small connection (well probably not small) but that connection will open the door for Christian men to be able to speak with young black men, even from that perspective I think they will be more willing to give them a shot, or just to listen, being that they can make that connection that this is a Christian man that made me want to stand up for my rights.

Herring: In thinking about the workshop and your experience growing up around Christian men, why do you think Christian men struggle so much with police or does their struggle or perception with police prevent them from communicating a more positive message. What I'm trying to get around to, if you think about the concepts, the principles of Christianity and Christ, shouldn't it be simple or easy that Christian men have or communicate to young men and even act toward authority in a different manner? If that is the case, why do Christian men struggle so much with police and authority, if you believe that.

Participant: Well, I guess from experiences I've had, even though a lot of the men I know are Christians, the older men still have that perception from back in the day of how police treated black men unfairly in the past, and a lot of them just can't get past that. I guess it's that fear of that distrust of police from way back (previous experiences) and they bring it with them, even though now they profess Christ, it's just still like a hurdle that a lot of them just don't get past.

Herring: Do you feel that, after the workshop and the series of things that have taken place in the church as a member with the bible studies and the preaching, do you feel that positive police relations can take place?

Participant: I think I do. Just as a man in general, hardworking man, police are hard working men just as I am, and a lot of things they do, they're trying to bring peace to the situations. And you're always going to have some who take it a bit far, but we have to remember that that's not all of them, and it's probably not the majority, but we have to give them the benefit of the doubt that they are here to bring peace, and they're working hard, and may be as fearful as we are in certain situations. I believe that I can speak with them and help them to see from that point of view that I was able to see from the conference, that these guys are working just as hard as we are, but they're faced with much greater danger than we could probably even imagine.

Herring: Thinking of the workshop and let's say if this was to be used to help bring knowledge to other men, what are some of the weaknesses, how do you think it needs to be strengthened, what would need to be changed about that workshop?

Participant: One thing could be, I guess, at this one that I attended, we didn't see uniformed cops, so maybe that could be a touch that could be added, when you actually hear from different uniformed cops or detectives, just hearing them bringing their point of view of their experiences to the light so that we can actually hear from them and try to see from their perspective. You can always use more participants, getting more younger black men to attend. I think that was two of the things that I could think of.

Herring: What will you tell your children about the police? So many of us grew up at an early age have been told negative things or distrust, but what will you tell them about police and their relations with police, especially knowing that they may encounter them in the wrong way (a negative encounter where the police is wrong). How might you start educating him?

Participant: I think some of the first things that I would teach my about police are the things that were taught to me, like police are here to protect and serve. We ask them to come into some of the most dangerous and worse situations, so we should give them respect. Just like with any man, you give respect to get respect, and keep in mind that their jobs are to go into the worst of situations and bring peace, we have to remember that they may be just as frightened or fearful as we are. So just keep that in mind. Always keep your hands where they can see them, and always be very respectful, even if you feel that they are not always in the right. You be respectful until you are in a position where you can get help from someone who can address that officer.

Herring: I appreciate you and your time so much. Are there any things that we did not cover, that you'd just like to share, or have closing thoughts or comments, that you might want to share, knowing that we're evaluating this workshop to see the value or impact that it might have. Anything on the workshop or any closing words?

Participant: I just think that it was a really good eye-opening workshop, and I'm looking forward to it expanding because I believe that it's really needed in this day and time because every day, not only are we having more and more bad encounters between young black males and police, but we're having so many encounters with kids and guns and we just need as much help as we can get in our communities and I believe that if we can ever get back that unity between black men and police, then a lot of our black men would live longer. So I'm really looking forward to this police and black men conference to really expand and take off, and I'm willing to do what I can to help it get there.

Herring: Excellent and that means a lot. Well I thank you so much for your time and your participation.

Participant: You're welcome.

APPENDIX G

E-MAIL INVITATION TO LAW ENFORCEMENT TO ATTEND ROUNDTABLE DISCUSSION

I AM THE FORMER police chief of Hartsville, SC, and Salisbury, NC. My career started in 1981 as a Chapel Hill public safety officer (attached you will find a copy of my vitae). Throughout my career I started and participated in a number of programs that focused on at risk youth including Volunteers for Youth, Durham Companions, Boys and Girls Club, and NC Tarheel Challenge Academy. Much of my career has also focused on programs and initiatives that strengthened relationships between the Black community and police. I currently serve as the executive director of the Institute for Homeland and Workforce Development and I am a professor in the Criminal Justice Department at NCCU.

The church I attend is hosting a second workshop that focuses on strengthening the relationship between Black men and police. Members live and work throughout the Research Triangle Park area. The concept is to educate and better inform men about ways they can serve as advocates to young Black males in an effort to strengthen the relationships between young Black males and police. Those who attended the first workshop all agreed it was a great success and there is a need for this kind of discussion. Officers did not attend the first session.

I am convening a few officers to have a structured dialogue session in a round-table atmosphere in which I will facilitate. Most of this small group of men (about 20) attended the previous workshop that focused on educating them on law enforcement and community relations. The workshop was and is hosted by the Men's Ministry at Cup of Salvation Deliverance Church and Ministries. The workshop is also in support of my dissertation for my Doctor of Ministry degree.

Can you recommend a couple of officers to participate in the discussion? Gender and race are not significant.

The primary focus is for the men to have a healthy discussion with police to improve the men's understanding of local law enforcement. Once again, the concept is to educate and better inform men about ways they can serve as advocates to young Black males in strengthening relationships among young Black males, police, and the criminal justice system.

The discussion will take place November 1, 2014 (Saturday) from 10:00 a.m. to 12:00 noon. Media will not be present, public recruitment will not take place, and the session will not be recorded.

I hope to have your support and look forward to your response. Thanks for all that you do!!!

APPENDIX H

ANNOTATED BIBLIOGRAPHY

MANY RESOURCES WERE reviewed for this project. Some were more greatly referenced then others. Below are a few select sources that were more heavily relied upon then others and may prove to be beneficial to some readers. They are divided into the categories of biblical, theological, historical, contemporary, and research.

BIBLICAL

Benning, Barry. *Jesus and Roman authority in Roman Influence on the Birth of Christianity.* http://www.barrybenning.com/roman_influence.pdf. n.d.

Benning provides documented perspectives that bring insight into how Jesus viewed Roman authority. Benning not only addresses Roman authority during the time of Christ, but also identifies the established Jewish religious order as a dominating authority. A major portion of his work focuses on the conflict between Roman authority and Jewish authority. As the recognized and formal civil authority, it was not unusual for Roman authority to meddle in the affairs of the Jewish people. This essay is discussed in Chapter 3: Foundations.

Campbell, Regi and Richard Chancy. *Mentor Like Jesus.* **Nashville, TN: B&H Publishing Group, 2009.**

The author uses Jesus as the greatest example of a mentor. The primary premise is that starting small mentoring groups can create major global changes. The author focuses on spiritual concepts of prayer, teaching, and service as a foundation for mentoring. Strengths of the book are its emphasis that it is not about the mentor, but rather society at large. Chapter One begins with an excellent focus on mentoring with a purpose. When encouraging Christian men to mentor during tough economic times that can create a life of major responsibilities and limited free time, Christian men must better understand the impact they can have on the world at large. This is especially true when changing the paradigm of Black males in the prison system. Information from this book is cited in the problem statement and used to inform the survey given to evaluate the workshop intervention.

Brand, Chad, Charles Draper, and Archie England. *Holman Illustrated Bible Dictionary.* **Nashville: Holman Bible Publishers, 2003.**

John McRay chronicles the history of Romans and the Roman Empire in the *Holman Illustrated Bible.*[155] According to McRay, the Roman Empire was born after the fall of the Republic of Rome government around 27 B.C. While the reasons for the fall of the Republic of Rome are not fully clear and complicated, some of the reasons include unrest among the classes, problems in maintaining order, and difficulty recruiting soldiers. Without question, Roman rule was oppressive, "Everything about Roman occupation was hateful to the Jews, from oppressive taxes to physical abuse by Roman soldiers to the repugnant idea that the Roman leader was a god."[156] This information is discussed in Chapter 3: Foundations.

---

155 John McRay. "How the Jews Lived in Jesus' Time." 2003. http://ancienthistory.about.com/od/biblicalhistory/a/How-the-Jews-Lived-in-Jesus-Time.htm.

156 Ibid.,1415.

Jensen, Irving. *Jensen's Survey of the Old Testament.* **Chicago: The Moody Bible Institute of Chicago, 1978.**

Jensen's work is well known for his survey of the Old and New Testaments. God had been acting among the people of the world centuries before Christ, and the Old Testament provides the historical setting of Christianity, serving as the Bible of Jesus.[157] The Old Testament provides documentation of religious, social, geographical, and political settings.[158] The first translation of the Old Testament was the Greek Septuagint (LXX, 70) and the English title Exodus has origins in the Greek Septuagint, which means departure, or exit.[159] These references are found in the Old Scripture foundation section.

MacArthur, John. *The MacArthur Bible Commentary: Unleashing God's Truth, One Verse at a Time.* **Nashville: Thomas Nelson Publishing Co., 2005.**

MacArthur provides commentary on various aspects of the Bible. The scripture discussed in Chapter 3: Foundations, the Old Testament section, comes from Exodus 2:11–15, as well as the expanded context of Exodus 2. Exodus gives a report of the first of God's deliverances of Israel as was promised to Abraham and is the second book of the Pentateuch. Moses is attributed with writing Exodus soon after the completion of the tabernacle as described in Exodus 35–40. This work is mentioned in Chapter 3: Foundations, the Old Testament section.

THEOLOGICAL

Hazle, Dave. "Practical Theology Today and the Implications for Mission." *International Review of Mission* **92, no. 366 (2003): 345.**

Hazle provides paradigms in which theology can be divided to provide an understanding of the overarching scope of practical theology. According to Hazle, practical theology has undergone a "rebirth" over the last three

---

157 Irving Jensen. *Jensen's Survey of the Old Testament.* Chicago: The Moody Bible Institute of Chicago, 1978, pg. 16.
158 Ibid,17.
159 Ibid, 25.

decades, first being concerned with equipping people for tasks such as preaching and pastoral care. Second, that rebirth has challenged the traditional methodologies of theological synthesis, developing socio-theological perspectives like political theology. His work is referenced in Chapter 3: Foundations, the Theological Foundation section.

Osmer, Richard R. *Practical Theology: An Introduction.* **William B. Eerdmans Publishing Co., 2008.**

Osmer provides a framework for analysis of practical theology. He uses a style of asking key questions that assist with comprehending the tasks of practical theology. His questions are used to frame how practical theology applies to this research project and how the church can be used to strengthen the relationship between Black men and police. Osmer's work is referenced in Chapter 3: Foundations, the Theological Foundation section.

Thurman, Howard. *Jesus and the Disinherited.* **Nashville: Abingdon, 1976.**

The forward of *Jesus and the Disinherited* begins with sharing the differences between Howard's work and liberation theology. Howard believes that Christians have been reluctant to examine hatred and have been rather sentimental in attempts to address hatred in human life. He believes that hatred destroys and self-love and love for others must take place for God's Kingdom of Justice to prevail. According to Howard, hatred cannot be defined, but it can be described and he provides four progressive elements of the description. Howard discusses how the New Testament may be read as a guide of resistance for the oppressed. Howard views Jesus as a partner in the struggles of the oppressed and his life exemplifies a solution. Hatred does not empower; it decays. Only through self-love and love of one another can God's justice prevail. This book is referenced in Chapter 3: Foundations, the Historical Foundation section.

Smith, R. Drew. *Long March Ahead: African American Churches and Public Policy in Post-Civil Rights America.* **Durham: Duke University Press, 2004.**

This edited book is the second volume of two and both volumes provide analysis of data received from surveying 1,956 black churches located in nineteen major cities throughout the nation and twenty-six small rural counties in the south. The goal of the project was to fill the gap in scholarly research related to Black church involvement in the political arena that goes beyond activism. Christopher Winship authored the essay, *End of a Miracle? Crime, Faith, and Partnership in Boston in the 1990s.* Some give credit to the significant decline in violence to a partnership between police and inner city Black ministers. Called the Ten Point Coalition, its focus was on youth violence. This edited book is referenced in the Chapter 3: Foundations, the Theological Foundation section.

HISTORICAL
LaFree, Gary, and Kriss Drass. "African American Collective Action & Crime, 1955–1991." ***Social Forces,*** **1997:835–853.**

Lafree and Drass studied the annual changes in Black civil rights-related collective action and Black and White arrest rates. The authors present four competing hypotheses on the relationships between rates of collective political action and crime during the postwar era. This information is referenced in Chapter 3: Foundations, the Historical Foundation section.[160]

Lewis, John, Andrew Aydin, and Nate Powell. "March: Book One." N.D.

It is not a new concept to solicit the church to engage its assistance in social justice issues and to address oppression and many other acts of institutional racism and injustice. The March on Washington arguably was a milestone for the Civil Rights Era, bringing together thousands of people with diverse backgrounds to the nation's capital. John Lewis was a key figure during this time and took a creative approach in sharing his biography, which bridged Christianity and social justice. His journey is referenced in Chapter 3: Foundations, Historical Foundation section.

---

160 Gary LaFree and Kriss Drass. "African American Collective Action & Crime, 1955–1991." *Social Forces,* 1997, pgs. 835–853.

CONTEMPORARY

Carter, David L. and Louis A. Radalet. *Police and the Community*. Michigan: Prentice Hall Publishing, 2001.

This book serves as a baseline book for lower level academic criminal justice programs. It provides a comprehensive introduction to community oriented policing (COP). COP's primary goal is to engage all citizens to assist with addressing issues of quality of life and crime in the community. It is one of the most significant recent trends in policing, and its related topics are central to the effective management of the Black male/police relationships. The book serves as an easy to read text that provides key research, concepts, and practices when it comes to engaging minority communities. This article is referenced in Chapter 3: Foundations, the Contemporary Foundation section.

Desmond, Scott A. and Kristopher H. Morgan. "Congregations and Crime: Is the Spatial Distribution of Congregations Associated with Neighborhood Crime Rates?" *Journal for the Scientific Study of Religion,"* 49, no. 1 (2010): 37–55.

This article researches the relationship between congregations and crime. It focuses at the micro neighborhood level on congregation involvement in the community, which is seldom done. The authors examined whether the presence of different types of congregations would influence different types of crime. The strength of the article is that it focuses on variables that are very seldom researched together. Black Protestants were isolated in the findings. Challenges with the article are that the sample is one city, Indianapolis, and the finding did not seem to be that significant. The relevance to this research project is bringing more insight into whether Christian mentors of young Black males will make a difference on crime in their community. This article is highlighted in the introduction of Chapter 1.

Dowler, Kenneth and Raymond Sparks. "Victimization, Contact with Police, and Neighborhood Conditions: Reconsidering African American and Hispanic Attitudes Toward the Police," *Police Practice and Research* 9, no. 5 (December 2008): 395–415.

The purpose of the study was to build on prior research. It examined minority attitudes toward police, while assessing the interaction effects of neighborhood context, victimization, contact with police, and community and police force characteristics. Strengths of the project are the scope of the data and sample size. Data was collected from a 1998 survey of twelve US cities. The US Bureau of Justice Statistics and the Office of Community Oriented Policing Services managed the project. One challenge of the work is that it is more than twelve years old. The research brings direct insight into Black males' perception of police. This work is cited in Chapter 3: Foundations, the Contemporary Foundation section.

Gabbidon, Shaun L. and Helen Taylor Greene. *Race and Crime.* **Thousand Oaks, CA: Sage Publications, Inc., 2005.**

The text provides an analysis of the issues of race and crime from a historical and contemporary context. It explores race and ethnicity on each of the major components of the criminal justice system. Strengths include an objective overview of topics such as collecting crime data to more subjective information on experiences of diverse racial groups. The text not only focuses on Blacks, but Asians, Latinos, and Native Americans, as well. The text serves as a strong foundation for synthesizing race and crime in the United States from the past to the "present." One challenge with the book is that it is dated 2005. This book was used to better understand definitions of race and is referenced in the Definitions section at the beginning of this book, and in Chapter 3: Foundations, the Theoretical Foundation section.

Gordon, Mary Beth. *Making the Match: Law Enforcement, the Faith Community and the Value-Based Initiative.* **Washington: US Department of Justice, Office of Community Oriented Policing Services, 2003.**

The US Department of Justice Office of Community Oriented Policing Services (COPS) has funded initiatives aimed at using faith organizations for strengthening relationships with police. The value-based initiative (VBI) is a COPS-funded strategy that emphasizes training and technical assistance for problem solving on a community level, through community-led initiatives that explore and promote what a community values most. The COPS office has expanded the VBI program to encourage law enforcement agencies to create or strengthen local projects that build trust between the police and their faith-based communities. Several initiatives bringing the faith community and law enforcement together were started throughout the United States. This article chronicles those initiatives and they are discussed in Chapter 3: Foundations, the Contemporary Foundation section.

Herring, Maulin C. *Destiny Denied: A Black Man's Prevention and Survival Guide to Police Encounters.* **Maulin C. Herring, 2011.**

The book uses a micro perspective that is based on the author's more than thirty years of experience in the criminal justice practitioner and academic arenas. Strengths include providing specific measures for Black males to use when approached by police in diverse settings. The author also brings insight into diverse police officers by categorizing them, challenging the premise that all police officers are the same. The book primarily focuses on changing the perceptions of both police and Black males when it comes to prejudging thoughts. One challenge of the text is that it is self-published. This book is referenced throughout the intervention workshop.

Meares, Tracey L. and Kelsi B. Corkan. "When 2 or 3 Come Together," *William and Mary Law Review* **48, no. 4 (2007): 1315–1387.**

This article is one of the very few that addresses issues related to churches, Blacks, and police. It is interesting that it was published in a law review journal. The researchers investigate policies that address disadvantaged urban neighborhoods from a community-based context. The data source is a community-wide prayer vigil held in Chicago in May of 1997. The vigil resulted from collaboration between the Chicago Police Department and hundreds of mostly African American churches on Chicago's West Side. A major question researched is, if collaboration between churches and the police, through religious activity, enhances community efficacy of poor minority neighborhoods, is there any way to reconcile the benefits of such activity with constitutional concerns about religious establishments? The focus is on the extent to which African Americans have been able to influence this jurisprudence through litigation, rather than the internal structure of establishment clause jurisprudence. While the purpose of the research is to address issues of the judicial branch, much insight is gathered from the data analysis that can assist local churches and police departments in improving relations in the Black community and controlling crime. This article is referenced and cited in the Introduction.

Birzer, Michael L. "What Makes a Good Police Officer? Phenomenological Reflections from the African-American Community." *Police Practice and Research* 9, No. 3 (July 2008): 199–212.

This research uses a phenomenological method to investigate two questions: (1) What are African Americans' perceptions of the police following contact with a police officer? and (2) What are the qualities that African Americans think are important for police officers to possess? Semistructured interviews over a three-month period with thirty-two African American participants were used for data collection. Not surprisingly, findings suggest that African Americans viewed their contact with police positively when the officer utilized human relations traits such as cultural sensitivity, empathy, and fairness. The paper provides a thorough review of the literature, which is helpful in finding related studies. More information could have been provided on the history of police community relations in the sample community. This article is discussed in Chapter Six, the conclusion.

Brunson, Rod K. and Ronald Weitzer. "Negotiating Unwelcome Police Encounters: the Intergenerational Transmission of Conduct Norms," *Journal of Contemporary Ethnography*, 40, no. 4 (2011): 425–456.

This research focuses on how people learn to manage potential encounters before police engagement. It brings insight into the premise that the church can play a role in influencing young Black males about their perceptions and responses to police encounters. While most research on police-citizen relations is centered on how police officers treat citizens, less research focuses on how citizens behave toward officers or how they may counsel others to behave if an officer stops them. This article examines an important way in which police encounters are structured, by the transmission of a set of conduct norms from one generation to the next. The research uses in-depth quality analysis and takes place in a city known for high crime and a strained relationship between the police and the community, East St. Louis, Illinois. This article is cited and used in the problem statement and used to develop the strategies recommended in the workshop, informing Black males on what to do when approached by police.

Stoddard, David A. and Robert Tamasy. *The Heart of Mentoring: Ten Proven Principles for Developing People to Their Fullest Potential.* **Colorado Springs, CO: Navpress, 2009.**

The authors provide insightful perspectives for the reader to use when gaining a better understanding of mentoring. The book focuses on mentoring as a lifelong commitment that should be done from the heart. The authors attempt to define mentoring and then provide chapters that challenge individuals to assess and develop motives for mentoring. From the authors' perspective, mentoring is a life journey that is pursued from the heart to influence others. One of the greatest strengths of the text comes at the end with the list of the ten powerful principles for effective mentoring. A weakness may be considered that it is from a micro-opinionated perspective of two individuals. The book helps in cases in which men do not see it as their responsibility to mentor others, and instead, view it as a task. This book is referenced in the problem statement and used to frame why it is important for Christian men to educate young Black males in the intervention workshop.

RESEARCH

Berg, Bruce. *Qualitative Research Methods For The Social Sciences.* **Boston: Pearson, 2007.**

Berg provides a comprehensive coverage of qualitative techniques in a way that is easy to understand and follow. The text provides guidance in ways of collecting and making sense of qualitative data. The text was used as a reference for developing the research design and analyzing data.

Bordens, Kenneth and Bruce Abbott. *Research Design and Methods: A Process Approach.* **Boston: McGraw-Hill, 2005.**

Bordens explores and discusses the research process, including getting and developing a research idea, designing and conducting a study, and analyzing and reporting data. A systematic overview of the research process is presented in an illustrative format. The author emphasizes the importance of ethical conduct in the treatment of research participants. The text was used as a reference for developing the research design and analyzing data.

ABOUT THE AUTHOR

Reverend Dr. Maulin C. Herring has over thirty-three years in the public safety field as a practitioner, professor, and consultant, progressing from public safety officer to police chief.

Herring serves as executive director of the Institute for Homeland Security and Workforce Development and a criminal justice visiting professor at North Carolina Central University. He has facilitated community policing workshops for the US Department of Justice and homeland security courses for the US Department of Homeland Security.

With twenty-seven years of college-level teaching experience in the disciplines of homeland security, fire services management, criminal justice, public administration, and sociology, Herring is the author of *Destiny Fulfilled: A Black Man's Prevention and Survival Guide to Police Encounters*.

Licensed as a minister of the Gospel in 2005 and ordained in 2007, he serves as a Pastor of International Ministries and Teaching and Discipleship. He is the executive vice-president of Outstretched Hands CDC, Inc.

BIBLIOGRAPHY

Akers, Ronald. *Criminological Theories: Introduction, Evaluation and Application.* Los Angeles: Roxbury, 2004.

———. "Social Learning Theory and Adolescent Cigarette Smoking." *Sociological Quarterly*, 1985: 625–663.

Alexander, Michelle. *The New Jim Crow: Mass Incarceration in the Age of Colorblindness.* 2011.

American Experience. "Freedom Riders: Threatened, Attacked, Jailed." http://www.pbs.org/wgbh/americanexperience/freedomriders/issues/victory-for-nonviolence (accessed November 25, 2014).

Anderson, Ray. *The Shape of Practical Theology: Empowering Ministry with Theological Praxis.* Downers Grove, IL: InterVarsity Press, 2001.

Anderson, T.W. and Jeremy Finn. *The New Statistical Analysis of Data.* New York: Springer, 1996.

Andrews, Alan. *The Kingdom Life: A Practical Theology of Discipleship and Spiritual Formation,* Colorado Springs, CO: NavaPress, 2010.

Authorities. Dictionary.com. *Collins English Dictionary: Complete & Unabridged 10th Edition.* HarperCollins Publishers. http://dictionary.reference.com/browse/authorities (accessed: November 09, 2014).

Babbie, Earl. *The Practice of Social Research.* Belmont: Wadsworth, 1986.

Benning, Barry. *http://www.barrybenning.com/roman_influence.pdf.* n.d. http://www.barrybenning.com/roman_influence.pdf.

Berg, Bruce. *Qualitative Research Methods for the Social Sciences.* Boston: Pearson, 2007.

Birzer, Michael L. "What Makes a Good Police Officer? Phenomenological Reflections from the African-American Community." *Police Practice and Research* 9, No. 3 (July 2008): 199–212.

Bordens, Kenneth and Bruce Abbott. *Research Design and Methods: A Process Approach.* Boston: McGraw-Hill, 2005.

Bowker, John. "Political theology." *The Concise Oxford Dictionary of World Religions.* 1997. Encyclopedia.com. (November 9, 2014). http://www.encyclopedia.com/doc/1O101-Politicaltheology.html.

Brand, Chad, Charles Draper, and Archie England. *Holman Illustrated Bible Dictionary.* Nashville: Holeman Bible Publishers, 2003.

Barclay, William. *The Gospel of Luke.* Louisville, KY: Westminster Press, 1975.

Browning, Don S. *A Fundamental Practical Theology: Descriptive and Strategic Proposals.* Minneapolis: Fortress Press, 1996. https://www.questia.com/read/119238259/a-fundamental-practical-theology-descriptive-and.

Brunson, Rod K. and Ronald Weitzer. "Negotiating Unwelcome Police Encounters: The Intergenerational Transmission of Conduct Norms." *Journal of Contemporary Ethnography* 40, No. 4 (2011): 425–456.

Bureau of Justice Statistics. Retrieved from http://www.bjs.gov/.

Butler, Trent C. Editor. Entry for "Authority." *Holman Bible Dictionary.* http://www.studylight.org/dictionaries/hbd/view.cgi?n=566. 1991.

Campbell, Regi and Richard Chancy. *Mentor Like Jesus.* Nashville, TN: B&H Publishing Group, 2009.

Carter, David L. *The Police and the Community.* Boston: Pearson, 2002.

Carter, David L. and Louis A. Radalet. *Police and the Community.* Michigan: Prentice Hall Publishing, 2001.

Chaney, Cassandra and Ray Robertson. "Racism and Police Brutality in America." *Journal of African American Studies*, 2013: 480–505.

Creswell, John W. *Research Design: Qualitative, Quantitative, and Mixed Methods Approaches.* Thousand Oaks: SAGE, 2003.

Crotty, Michael J. *The Foundations of Social Research: Meaning and Perspective in the Research Process.* Thousand Oaks: SAGE, 1998.

Cup of Salvation website. Retrieved from http://cupofsalvation.org/.

Dashner, Terry. "Jesus' Views on Civil Government." Broken Arrow: GoArticles.com, October 5, 2005.

Dowler, Kenneth and Raymond Sparks. "Victimization, Contact with Police, and Neighborhood Conditions: Reconsidering African American and Hispanic Attitudes Toward the Police." *Police Practice And Research* 9, No. 5 (December 2008): 395–415.

Dunham, Roger G. and Geoffrey P. Alpert. *Critical Issues In Policing: Contemporary Readings.* Long Grove, IL: Waveland Press, Inc., 2010.

Ellis, Carl, Jr. *Free at Last: The Gospel in the African American Experience.* Downers Grove, IL: Intervarsity Press, 1996.

Engel, Robin. "Citizens' Perceptions of Distributive and Procedural Injustice During Traffic Stops With Police." *Journal of Research in Crime and Delinquency*, 2005: 445–481.

"Final Plans for the March on Washington for Jobs and Freedom," Organizing Manual No. 2. 1963.

Gabbidon, Shaun L. and Helen Taylor Greene. *Race and Crime*. Thousand Oaks, CA: Sage Publications, Inc., 2005.

Gang Reduction Strategy Steering Committee, "2012 Youth and Crime Community Indicator Report." Retrieved from http: //dconc.gov/government/departments-a-e/criminal-justice-resource-center/gang-reduction-strategy.

Gordon, Mary Beth. *Making the Match: Law Enforcement, the Faith Community and the Value-Based Initiative*. Washington: US Department of Justice, Office of Community Oriented Policing Services, 2003.

Gronberg, Ray. *Blacks Suffer Disproportionately from Crime*. Retrieved from http://www.heraldsun.com/news/x112098135/Blacks-suffer-disproportionately-from-crime-police-say.

Harrison, Paige M. and Allen J. Beck. *Bureau of Justice Statistics Bulletin: Prisoners In 2005*. 2006. Http://Www.Ojp.Usdoj.Gov/Bjs/Abstract/P05.Htm (Accessed April 19, 2007).

Hazle, Dave. "Practical Theology Today and the Implications for Mission." *International Review of Mission* 92, no. 366 (2003): 345. https://www.questia.com/read/1G1-107761086/practical-theology-today-and-the-implications-for.

Hemmens, Craig and Daniel Levin. "Resistance is Futile: The Right to Resist Unlawful Arrest in an Era of Aggressive Policing." *Crime and Delinquency*, 2000: 472–496.

Hermans, Chris and Mary Elizabeth Moore, "Chapter One: The Contribution of Empirical Theology by Johannes A. Van Der Ven: An Introduction," in *Hermeneutics and Empirical Research in Practical Theology: The Contribution of Empirical Theology by Johannes A. Van Der Ven*, ed. Chris A. M. Hermans and Mary E. Moore. Boston: Brill, 2004, 3, https://www.questia.com/read/117547298.

Hendricks, Obery. *The Politics of Jesus.* Garden City: Doubleday, 2006.

Henry, Matthew. *Matthew Henry's Commentary on the Whole Bible: Complete and Unabridged in One Volume.* Peabody: Hendrickson Publishers, 2008.

Herring, Maulin C. *Destiny Denied: A Black Man's Prevention and Survival Guide To Police Encounters.* Durham, NC: Maulin C. Herring, 2011.

Jensen, Irving. *Jensen's Survey of the New Testament.* Chicago: The Moody Bible Institute of Chicago, 1981.

Jensen, Irving. *Jensen's Survey of the Old Testament.* Chicago: The Moody Bible Institute of Chicago, 1978.

Johnson, Byron R. *The Role of African-American Churches in Reducing Crime Among Black Youth.* Philadelphia: Manhattan Institute, 2001.

Jones-Brown, Delores D. "Debunking the Myth of Officer Friendly." *Journal of Contemporary Criminal Justice*, 2000: 209–229.

Kendall, Diana. *Sociology in Our Times: The Essentials.* Independence: Thomson-Wadsworth, 2006.

Kirsch, Johnathan. *Moses: A Life.* New York: Ballantine Books, 1998.

LaFree, Gary, and Kriss Drass. "African American Collective Action & Crime, 1955–1991." *Social Forces,* 1997:835–853.

Leedy, Paul D. and Jeanne E. Ormrod. *Practical Research: Planning and Design.* Upper Saddle River: Pearson, 2005.

Lewis, John, Andrew Aydin, and Nate Powell. *March: Book One.* Marietta, Ga: Top Shelf Productions, 2013.

Liska, Ailen A. *Perspectives on Deviance.* Englewood Cliffs: Prentice-Hall, 1987.

Lundman, Richard. "Driver Race, Ethnicity, and Gender and Citizen Reports of Vehicle Searches by Police and Search Hits: Toward A Triangulated Scholarly Understanding." *The Journal of Criminal Law and Delinquency,* 2004: 309–345.

Mandela, Nelson. *Long Walk to Freedom: The Autobiography of Nelson Mandela.* Boston: Back Bay Books, 1995.

Matsueda, Ross. "The Current State Of Differential Association theory." *Crime and Delinquency,* 1988: 277–306.

MacArthur, John. *The MacArthur Bible Commentary: Unleashing God's Truth, One Verse at a Time.* Nashville: Thomas Nelson Publishing Co., 2005.

McRay, John. "How the Jews Lived in Jesus' Time." 2003. http://ancienthistory.about.com/od/biblicalhistory/a/How-the-Jews-Lived-in-Jesus-Time.htm.

Meares, Tracey L. and Kelsi B. Corkan. "When 2 Or 3 Come Together." *William And Mary Law Review* 48, No. 4 (2007): 1315–1387.

Mertens, Donna. *Research and Evalution in Education and Psychology.* Thousand Oaks: SAGE, 2005.

Miller, Joel, Robert Davis, Nicole Henderson, John Markovic, and Christopher Oritz. "Measuring Influences on Public Opinion of the Police Suing Time Series Data: Results of a Pilot Study." *Police Quarterly*, 2005: 394–401.

Miller-McLemore, Bonnie J. *The Wiley-Blackwell Companion to Practical Theology.* Malden, MA: Wiley-Blackwell, 2012. https://www.questia.com/read/123526761/the-wiley-blackwell-companion-to-practical-theology.

Newsome, James D. *Greeks, Romans, Jews—Currents of Culture and Belief in the New Testament World. Norcross GA:* Trininty Press International 1992.

Osmer, Richard R. *Practical Theology: An Introduction.* Grand Rapids, MI: William B. Eerdmans Publishing Co., 2008.

Peek, Charles, George Lowe, and Jon Alston. "Race and Attitudes toward Local Police: Another Look." *Journal of Black Studies*, 1981: 361–374.

Question Pro. *On-Line Research Made Easy.* ND. Http://Www.Questionpro.Com/Help/130-Inline.Html (Accessed May 13, 2007).

Robinson, B. F.. (1941). The Sociology of Race Riots. *Phylon (1940-1956), 2*(2), 162–171. http://doi.org/10.2307/271786

Robinson, Cleveland and Bayard Rustin. "Final Plans for the March on Washington for Jobs and Freedom." New York, 1963.

Scott, Desmond A. and Kristopher H. Morgan. "Congregations and Crime: Is the Spatial Distribution of Congregations Associated with Neighborhood Crime Rates?" *Journal for the Scientific Study of Religion* 49, No. 1 (2010): 37–55.

Selby, Donald J. *Introduction to the New Testament: The Word Became Flesh.* Wichita: Macmillan Publishing, 1971.

Smith, R. Drew. *Long March Ahead: African American Churches and Public Policy in Post-Civil Rights America.* Durham: Duke University Press, 2004.

Stoddard, David A. and Robert Tamasy. *The Heart of Mentoring: Ten Proven Principles for Developing People to Their Fullest Potential.* Colorado Springs, CO: Navpress, 2010.

Tannehill, Robert. *The Narrative Unity of Luke—Acts: A Literary Interpretation.* Minneapolis: Augsburg Fortress, 1990.

Taslitz, Andrew E. "Respect and the Fourth Amendment." *The Journal of Law & Criminology*, 2003: 15–101.

The Association of Practical Theology. Retrieved from http://practicaltheology.org/ on November 5, 2014.

Thurman, Howard. *Jesus and the Disinherited.* Boston: Beacon Press, 1996.

Tyler, Tom. "Policing in Black and White: Ethnic Grop Differences in Trust and Confidence in the Police." *Police Quarterly*, 2005: 322–342.

Veling, Terry A. *Practical Theology: On Earth as It Is in Heaven.* Maryknoll, NY: Orbis Books, 2005.

Viki, G. Tendayi, Michelle J. Culmer, Anja Eller, and Dominic Abrams. "Race and Willingness to Cooperate With the Police: The Roles of Quality of Contact, Attitudes Towards the Behavior and Subjective Norms." *British Journal of Social Psychology*, 2006: 285–302.

Walker, Samuel and Carol A. Archbold. *The New World of Police Accountability*. Thousand Oaks, CA: Sage Publications, Inc., 2014.

Weitzer, Ronald and Steven Tuch. "Race, Class and Perceptions of Discrimination of Police." 1999: 494–507.

Winship, Christopher. "End of a Miracle? Crime, Faith, and Partnership in Boston in the 1990s." In *Long March Ahead*, by R. Drew Smith, 171–192. Durham and London: Duke University Press, 2004.

WNCN. "Durham mayor: Racial profiling report will not be gathering dust." Retrieved from http://www.wncn.com/story/25594185/durham-city-council-reviews-findings-of-racial-profiling-report.

Woods, William K. and Edward Burdell. *A Survey of Racial Attitudes in Cincinnati: A Preliminary Report*. Cincinnati: Applied Information Resources of Cincinnati, OH, 2006.

Made in the USA
Charleston, SC
30 April 2016